Language Development

Activities for Home

Marion Nash and Jackie Lowe

 **David Fulton** Publishers

David Fulton Publishers Ltd
The Chiswick Centre, 414 Chiswick High Road, London W4 5TF

www.fultonpublishers.co.uk

First published in Great Britain by David Fulton Publishers 2004

David Fulton Publishers is a division of Granada Learning Limited, part of Granada plc.

British Library Cataloguing in Publication Data
A catalogue record for this book is available from the British Library.

ISBN 1–84312–170–0

Typeset by FiSH Books, London
Printed and bound in Great Britain

Contents

Background   vii

Acknowledgements   ix

Using the handbook   xi

Early Years/Nursery

Page	Session	Activity	Covering aim
1	1	Play the hiding under game	– Understanding the word *under*
3	2	Play the listening game	– Introducing listening skills
5	3	Play the moving over game	– Using the word *over*
7	4	Play the standing on game	– Understanding the word *on*
9	5	Play the big and little game	– Understanding the words *big* and *little*
11	6	Play the under game	– Using the word *under*
13	7	Play the up and down game	– Using the words *up* and *down*
15	8	Play the on and under game	– Understanding the words *on* and *under*
17	9	Play another listening game	– More listening skills
19	10	Play the listen and do game	– Listening and acting on instructions
21	11	Play the making different sounds game	– Recognising long/short speech sounds
23	12	Play the top and bottom game	– Understanding the words *top* and *bottom*

Foundation/Key Stage 1

Page	Session	Activity	Covering aim
25	1	Play the taking turns game	– Turn-taking
27	2	Play the happy and sad game	– Using and understanding the words *happy* and *sad*
29	3	The rhyming words game	– Using rhyming words
31	4	The hiding game: behind	– Understanding the word *behind*
33	5	The hiding game: in front	– Understanding the words *in front*
35	6	Play the hiding game	– Using the words *behind* and *in front*
37	7	Sounds and words	– Initial sounds *S* and *P*: building vocabulary
39	8	The question game: Who?	– Exploring questions: *Who?*
41	9	The middle game	– Using the word *middle*
43	10	The question game: Where?	– Exploring questions: *Where?*
45	11	Exploring feeling words	– Understanding the words *happy*, *sad* and *frightened*
47	12	More middle games	– Exploring different uses of words for *middle*

Key Stage 2

Page	*Session*	*Activity*	*Covering aim*
49	13	Play the tapping the beat game	– Tapping the beat
51	14	More beat tapping: guess the object game	– Beat tapping and guessing
53	15	Storylines	– Making stories
55	16	Listen, remember and do games	– Listening, remembering and doing
56	17	Sequencing life events	– Remembering and telling
57	18	The question game: When?	– Using the word *when*
59	19	Exploring feeling words	– Using the word *worried*
61	20	Rhyming word games	– Using rhyming words
63	21	Play the story game	– Telling a story
65	22	The word pair game	– Finding rhyming pairs
66	23	Now you tell me a story	– Retelling a story
68	24	Exploring feelings	– Explaining feelings in a story

| 69 | Record sheets |
| 72 | Songs and rhymes |

To our parents, and to parents and carers everywhere

Background

This book of ideas arose from implementing the Spirals Language Development course in nurseries and schools. (See page 72 for details of this book.) Parents often express a wish to help their children with activities at home which are effective, but also achievable in a busy lifestyle.

Myself and Jackie felt that there was a need for a handbook of simple, very achievable, play-based activities which teachers would feel happy to suggest to busy parents/carers and support workers. An easy-to-follow, photocopiable sheet would give guidance and act as a visual reminder of what to do.

We took just one key idea from each weekly session and built up a bank of effective learning experiences which could be provided at home to support the work in nursery or school, and to empower parents to work in collaboration with their children's setting. The handbook can also stand alone in providing ideas for teachers, speech and language therapists and parents.

Marion Nash

Acknowledgements

The publication of this book has been made possible by the foresight and support of the people who work in Plymouth Education Authority and those who direct it. The work has been supported and encouraged by Plymouth's Psychological Service.

We must also acknowledge and thank those parents who worked with us in supporting the Spirals approach and inspiring us to write these activities for home.

Using the handbook

The ideas in this book are linked directly to the 36 sessions in the book *Language Development: Circle Time Sessions to Improve Communications Skills*, which underpins the Spirals course.

Each page is designed to be used as a stand-alone handout to develop one key idea in a simple and user-friendly way. Parents and carers can use the ideas as play activities with their children at home.

The illustrations may also be given to act as a prompt for parents whose literacy skills are weak, or for whom English is an additional language. Coloured in and pinned to a wall at home, they also act as a visual reminder of simple games that can continue to be fun for all members of the family.

The aim is that one sheet will be given out <u>after</u> each session to reinforce concepts which have been introduced in that session. Active use of these sheets at home will further accelerate the children's learning and understanding, and encourage parents' involvement in establishing a powerful bedrock for learning. Using these sheets will empower parents to work in collaboration with their child's setting and give them confidence that they are 'doing the right thing'.

The grid on each page is for the parent to indicate how the activity went – did it go very well, with the child enjoying it and showing by the end that he or she had understood the word and concept? The empty boxes are for the parent to tick and/or date each time they try the activity. If the sheets are handed in after use, this device can help the teacher to understand how much support is being offered at home: it can also act as a motivator for parents and carers.

Date	☺ Comment

Date	☺ Comment
4/5/04	Jason likes this
5/5/04	game. His sister
7/5/04	joined in. ☺

The worksheets in this book may also be used independently where necessary, to give support in particular areas of language development. The record sheets at the end of the book can be used by parents and/or teachers to keep track of activities used.

The traditional songs and rhymes are also provided as a resource for parents and carers who may have forgotten the words!

Ideas for Home

Play the hiding under game

Early Years/Nursery Session 1: Understanding the word <u>under</u>

Date:...........

Get your child's *duvet* or sheet, put it on the floor and ask them to go *under* it.

Say, 'You are *under* the duvet.' Take a turn yourself to sit under the duvet/sheet. Say, 'I'm *under* too.'

Use the word 'under' and show your child things *under* as much as you can this week.

Date	☺ Comment

Under

Ideas for Home

Play the listening game

Early Years/Nursery Session 2: Introducing listening skills

Date:.............

Talk to your child about their ears. Ask, 'What do you use your ears for?' Help them to use the word 'listening'.

Next, turn off the television and sit quietly and listen together to all the noises you can hear.

Say, 'I am *listening* with my ears and I can hear...' – examples might be the clock ticking, tap dripping, gas fire humming, other children playing. Say, 'You are *listening* with your ears. What can you hear?'

Encourage your child to listen to noises inside the house (as above) and outside – examples might be traffic noises, birdsong, wind, rain. Say, 'You are listening with your ears. Let's listen with our ears – what can we hear?'

If you have time, play this listening game anywhere – in the car, on the bus, walking on the road, in the supermarket queue.

Date	☺ Comment

Listening

Ideas for Home

Play the moving over game

Early Years/Nursery Session 3: Using the word <u>over</u>

Date:............

Put a magazine, scarf, rug or newspaper on the floor. Hold your child's hand and walk slowly over the rug and say, 'We are walking *over* the scarf/rug.' Repeat this two or three times.

You want to teach your child the word 'over' and what it means. Continue by playing games – hopping over, jumping over, crawling over, tiptoeing over.

Encourage your child to say, 'I'm going *over*.'

Ask your child, 'Can you walk *over* the rug?' Take a turn and let your child ask you.

Use the word 'over' as much as you can during the week.

Date	☺ Comment

Over

Ideas for Home

Play the standing on game

Early Years/Nursery Session 4: Understanding the word <u>on</u>

Date:...........

Think of all the things your child can stand *on* in your house. Holding your child's hand do a little trail through the house seeing what you can stand on.

Say,   'We are standing *on* the mat.'
         'We are standing *on* the stairs.'
         'We are standing *on* the toybox.'

Put your child *on* a chair.
Say, 'You are standing *on* the chair.'

Play as many games as you can using the word 'on' and helping your child to say that word.

Date	☺ Comment

On

Ideas for Home

Play the big and little game

Early Years/Nursery Session 5: Understanding the words <u>big</u> and <u>little</u>

Date:............

Outside, look around for the biggest thing you can see; this may be a building or a tree, a lorry, a bus. Bring your child's attention to this thing by pointing to it, and say, 'That is *big*.' Do this several times.

Then look around for the smallest thing you can see; this may be a stone, a feather, a leaf, a blade of grass. Bring your child's attention to this and say, 'That is *little*.'

Do this with several things. Look together to see what else you can find that is *big*. See if you can find three things. Look together to see what you can find that is *little*. Collect three little things and say 'Yes, these are *little*.'

Talk about the *little* and *big* things at home. Find a little spoon and a big spoon, a little sock and a big sock, a little pan and a big pan, and so on.

Date	☺ Comment

Big and little

Ideas for home

Play the under game

Early Years/Nursery Session 6: Using the word <u>under</u>

Date:............

Get a tea-cloth or towel and two objects – a spoon and cup, or a teddy and toy car.

Spread the tea-cloth on the floor.
Put one object under the cloth – say, 'I'm putting the spoon *under* the cloth.' Ask your child, 'Where is the spoon?' If they say, 'There' you say, 'Yes, *under* the cloth'. Then ask your child, 'Can you put the cup *under* the cloth?'

Ask, 'Where is it?' Encourage them to say 'Under'. Play games asking your child to put things under. For example, 'teddy under the bed', 'the toothbrush under the towel'. Ask your child to tell you where the object is.

Date	☺ Comment

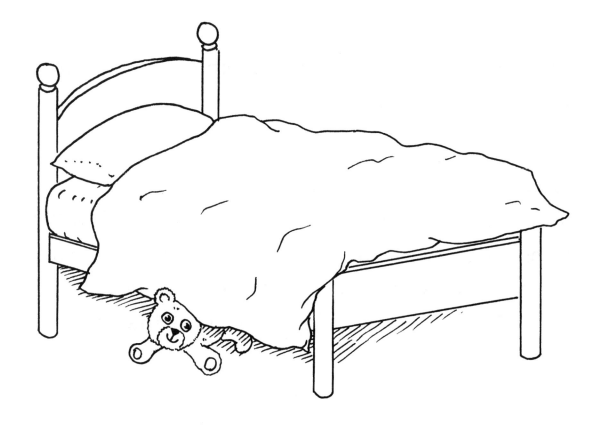

Under

Ideas for Home

Play the up and down game

Early Years/Nursery Session 7: Using the words <u>up</u> and <u>down</u>

Date:............

Stretch up high with your child and say, 'Up, up, up high' or sing a little song about 'up'. Bend down low with them and say, 'Down, down, down low' or sing a song about 'down'.

Hold a teddy bear or car *up* high and say, 'Teddy's *up* high.' Hold a teddy or car *down* low and say, 'Teddy's *down* low.'

Hold a toy up high and let your child see it. Say, 'I can see the car *up* high. Where is it?' Then bring it down and say, 'It's coming *down* now.'

Date	☺ Comment

13

Up and down

Ideas for Home

Play the on and under game

Early Years/Nursery Session 8: Understanding the words <u>on</u> and <u>under</u>

Date:...........

Take a small tea-cloth and a few objects; for example, a teddy bear/car/spoon/key/doll.

Lay the tea-cloth out flat and put one of the toys, e.g. the teddy, on the cloth. Say, 'The teddy's *on* the cloth.'

Then put one of the toys under the cloth and say, 'The car is *under* the cloth.'

Take them away, and then ask your child to put the key *on* the cloth – give him or her lots of praise for trying and say, 'It's *on* the cloth.' (If he or she gets it wrong just take it and put it in the right place saying, 'Now it's *on* the cloth!')

Next ask your child to put the spoon *under* the cloth – give lots of praise. If they get it wrong, put it under the cloth for them.

Play as many games as you can, asking your child to put things *under/on* things.

Take turns and encourage your child to ask you to place things.

Date	☺ Comment

15

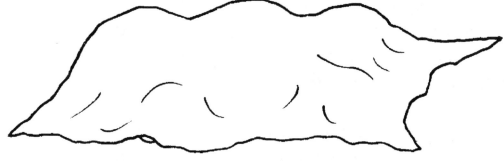

On and under

Ideas for home

Play another listening game

Early Years/Nursery Session 9: More listening skills

Date:............

Prepare three or four things to listen to.

Ideas: Cornflakes in a box
           Small bottle with water in it
           A cup with a teaspoon in it
           Piece of paper for screwing up.

Talk as you did in Session 2 about your child's ears and how they help you listen.

Encourage your child to listen to the sounds as you shake the cornflakes box, rattle the spoon in the cup, rustle the paper.

Then ask your child to close their eyes and turn around (so they can't peep) while you make *one* of the sounds. See if they can guess without looking which one it is, e.g. 'the spoon and cup' or 'cornflakes in a box'.

If you have time, take it in turns and you be the listener.

Date	☺ Comment

 Listening

Ideas for Home

Play the listen and do game

Early Years/Nursery Session 10: Listening and acting on instructions

Date:............

Tell your child you're going to play a game and they need to use their ears to listen. Make sure your child is looking at you. Tell your child that looking at people helps you to listen.

With your child, do the following things and ask your child to copy you. Say the words at the same time.

Touch your ears
Touch your nose
Touch your toes
Hands behind your head
Touch your eyebrows
Hands behind your back
Touch your shoulders

Start off slowly. Now ask your child to listen to you when you tell them to do these things and see if they can do them on their own. As they get the hang of it go faster and faster.

Play this game any time you can. Make it fun!

Date	☺ Comment

Listening and **doing**

Ideas for Home

Play the making different sounds game

Early Years/Nursery Session 11: Recognising long/short speech sounds

Date:............

Say to your child, 'I'm going to make a long, long sound that can go on forever – listen – you make a *ssssss* sound' (don't say the *name* of the letter – make the *sound*).

Say to your child, 'I'm going to make a short sound *t,t,t* (don't say the *name* of the letter – make the *sound*).

See if your child can make these sounds with you and talk about long and short sounds.

Play with some more sounds together and decide together which ones are long (*sh, f, th, m*) and which are short (*t, p*).

Date	☺ Comment

Long and **short** sounds

Ideas for home

Play the top and bottom game

Early Years/Nursery Session 12: Understanding the words <u>top</u> and <u>bottom</u>

Date:............

With your child look at a bottle together and decide which is the *bottom* and which is the *top*.

Look at a saucepan together and decide which is *top* and *bottom*. Use the words 'top' and 'bottom'.

Then if you have stairs or steps take your child to the bottom of the stairs and say, 'This is the *bottom* of the stairs. Where is the *top*?' Walk up the stairs with your child and say, 'This is the *top* of the stairs. Where is the *bottom* of the stairs?'

Play a game encouraging your child to put teddy at the top and the bottom of the stairs.

Date	☺ Comment

Top and bottom

Ideas for Home

Play the taking turns game

Foundation/Key Stage 1 Session 1: Turn-taking

Date:............

Talk to your child about *taking turns*.

Get a large soft ball and sit on the floor with your child. Say, 'We need to take turns to play this game. We are going to roll the ball to each other.'

Say, 'My turn', then roll the ball to the child and say, 'Your turn.' Praise your child for waiting his turn and listening.

If you have time, play a more active game taking turns:

'My turn to hop'
'Your turn to hop'
'My turn to jump'
'Your turn to jump.'

Praise your child for taking their turn and waiting for their turn.

Date	☺ Comment

Taking turns

Ideas for Home

Play the happy and sad game

Foundation/Key Stage 1 Session 2: Using and understanding the words <u>happy</u> and <u>sad</u>

Date:............

Play the happy and sad game. Notice when your child seems happy or sad. Talk to them about this using the words 'You're *happy* now' when your child is on the swing, watching TV, eating, playing, and 'You're *sad* now' if they seem sad.

Talk to your child about simple things that make you happy or sad. Find times in the day to say, for example, 'I feel *happy* today because the sun's out', or 'I feel *sad* today because it's raining and we can't go outside to play.'

Carry on during the week reinforcing the use of the words 'happy' and 'sad'.

Date	☺ Comment

27

Happy and sad

Ideas for Home

The rhyming words game

Foundation/Key Stage 1 Session 3: Using rhyming words

Date:............

Sing this rhyme with your child. Make it an action game by pointing to parts of the body as you sing.

Heads, shoulders, knees and toes, knees and toes.
Heads, shoulders, knees and toes, knees and toes.
Eyes and ears and mouth and nose,
Head, shoulders, knees and toes, knees and toes.

Say 'nose, toes' in a sing-song voice again: 'Nose, toes, your nose and toes end with the same sound.'

Sing the song again.

Say, 'Nose, toes, the words end with the same sound. They *Rhyme*.' During the week, try to find other words that rhyme: cat, mat, hat. Play games finding rhymes; for example, words that rhyme with their names (Jack, back). Also things you can see every day in and around the house; for example, egg, peg/tree, bee. Think of funny ones if you can.

Date	☺ Comment

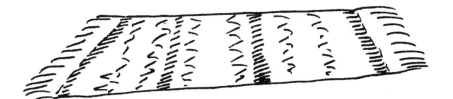

Rhyming

Ideas for Home

Play the hiding game: behind

**Foundation/Key Stage 1 Session 4: Understanding the word
behind**

Date:............

Take out one of your child's toys so they can see you
put it behind a cereal box, but where they can't see it.
Stand with your child and share with them that it is
now hidden. Say, 'It's hidden *behind* the box.' Fetch the
toy from behind the box and hide it behind something
else. Say, 'It's *behind* the...'.

During the week, notice and talk to your child about one
thing being behind another; for example, the tea-bags
behind the sugar. Use the word '*behind*' as often as you
can.

You can ask your child to stand behind you or behind
the television – help your child if they get muddled up.

Date	☺ Comment

Behind

Ideas for Home

Play the hiding game: in front

Foundation/Key Stage 1 Session 5: Understanding the words <u>in</u> <u>front</u>

Date:...........

Take one of your child's toys and put it in front of a cereal box. Say to your child, 'The teddy is *in front* of the box.' Take some other toys and put them in front of objects around the house. Emphasise each time that the toys are *in front*. Use the words 'in front' as much as you can.

Through the week put objects or toys in front of things around the house. Ask your child to stand in front of you and stand in front of the sofa. Help your child if they get muddled up.

Date	☺ Comment

In front

Ideas for Home

Play the hiding game

Foundation/Key Stage 1 Session 6: using the words <u>behind</u> and <u>in front</u>

Date:...........

Play a game with your child asking them to stand behind or in front of different things around the house. Then encourage your child to say to *you*, for example, 'Mummy, stand *behind* the television.' You can involve other adults in the house and make it fun.

Then move on to playing this game with objects and toys, using the words *behind, in front, in, on* and *under*. Make sure that your child is using these words.

If you want to, you can get a big cardboard box from the supermarket and play this game with your child. Encourage them to use the words *in, on, under, in front* and *behind*.

Date	😊 Comment

Behind and front

Ideas for Home

Sounds and words

Foundation/Key Stage 1 Session 7: Initial sounds S and P: building vocabulary

Date:............

Walk around your house with your child; collect in a bag all the objects you can find that begin with 's'; for example, sellotape, soap, scissors, sock. Put them on the table and see if your child knows the names of the objects.

Repeat on another day with objects that begin with the 'p' sound; for example, pen, pin, pan, plasticine.

Play putting the objects into two piles, one pile with words that start with the 's' sound, the other that start with the 'p' sound. Spend some time seeing if your child can find things that can be added to each of these piles. Pictures from magazines and catalogues may be cut out and put in the piles.

You can make a little book together with these pictures if you wish.

Date	☺ Comment

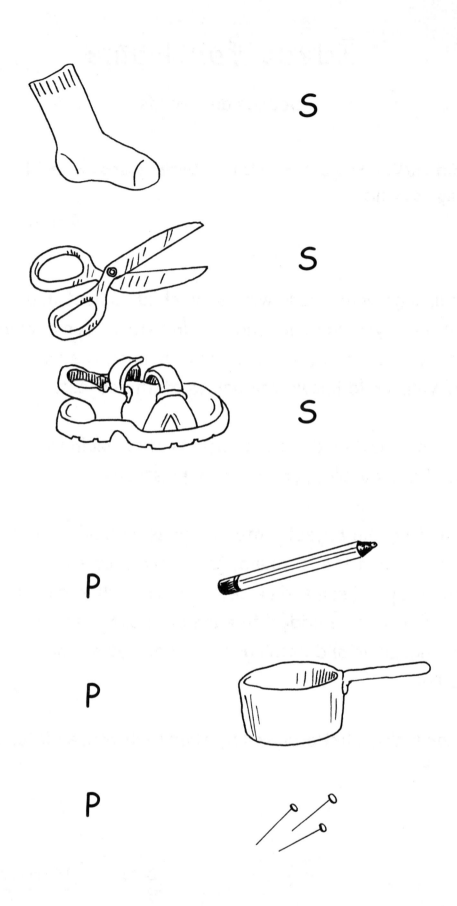

S

S

S

P

P

P

S and P

Ideas for Home

The question game: Who?

Foundation/Key Stage 1 Session 8: Who? questions

Date:............

During the week when you talk with your child use the question word *who*, and say a little about what that means.

For example: 'Who is at the door?' 'Who likes milk?' 'Who is the tallest?' 'Who is happy?'

Help your child to understand what it is you mean by the question 'who?' by giving them the answer first; for example, 'Who's at the door – it's Grandma!'

Look at a picture showing people doing things, and ask your child, 'Who is playing, shopping, driving?'

The next step may be more difficult for your child. Encourage them to ask you a question using the word 'who'; for example, 'Who is sitting down?'

Date	☺ Comment

Who?

Ideas for Home

The middle game

Foundation/Key Stage 1 Session 9: using the word <u>middle</u>

Date:............

Talk to your child about what we mean by *middle*. Place three cushions on the floor and sit on the middle one with your child. Say, 'We're sitting on the cushion in the middle.' Stand up and walk around the cushions, then ask, 'Can you sit on the cushion in the middle?' Get your child to help you change the cushions around and ask them again, 'Can you sit on the cushion in the middle?' Give them lots of praise if they get it right.

Play lots of games where your child has to find the middle object of three.

You could hide a treat in a middle pot or under a middle cup.

Get three differently coloured pots. Put two of the pots down and say to your child, 'Put this one in the middle.'

Move from three objects to five objects and help your child to find the middle one.

Date	☺ Comment

Middle

Ideas for Home

The question game: Where?

Foundation/Key Stage 1 Session 10: 'Where' questions?

Date:.............

During the week play the *where* question game. Ask your child, 'Where is teddy?', and then answer for them: 'He's under the bed.'

Before you go out somewhere ask your child, 'Where are we going?', and then give the answer: 'We're going to Playgroup'.

Find as many opportunities as possible during the week to encourage your child to ask 'Where' questions.

Date	☺ Comment

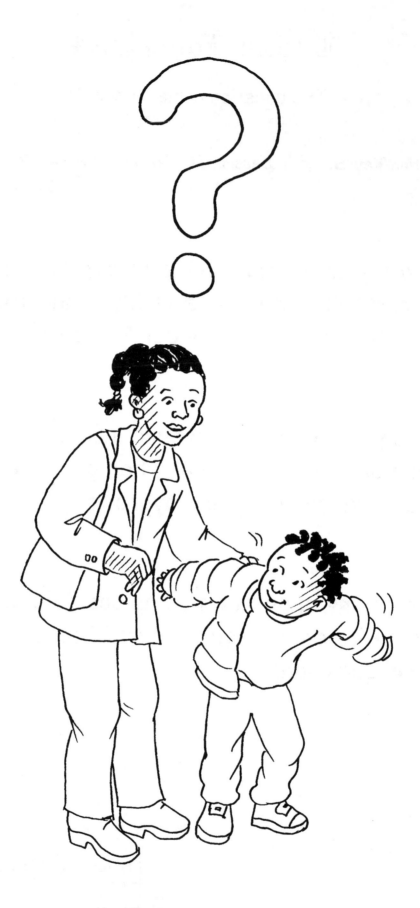

Where?

Ideas for Home

Exploring feeling words

Foundation/Key Stage 1 Session 11: understanding the words <u>happy</u>, <u>sad</u> and <u>frightened</u>

Date:...........

Play a game with your child about what makes them feel *happy*:

'I feel *happy* when... it's pizza for tea.'

'I feel *sad* when... we have to leave our friends.'

Then introduce *frightened*:

Talk about a situation when your child may be frightened; for example, a big dog comes up to them, or they hear a loud noise.

Encourage your child to relate the word 'frightened' to events that happen to them.

Date	☺ Comment

Feelings

Ideas for Home

More middle games

Foundation/Key Stage 1 Session 12: Exploring different uses of words for <u>middle</u>

Date:............

Stand with your child in the middle of the carpet. Say to your child, 'We are in the *middle* or *centre* of the carpet.'

Make a circle with rope, string or wool and ask your child to stand in the middle of the circle. Ask your child to hop in the middle or jump to the middle.

Draw a circle and ask your child to make a cross in the centre.

Date	☺ Comment

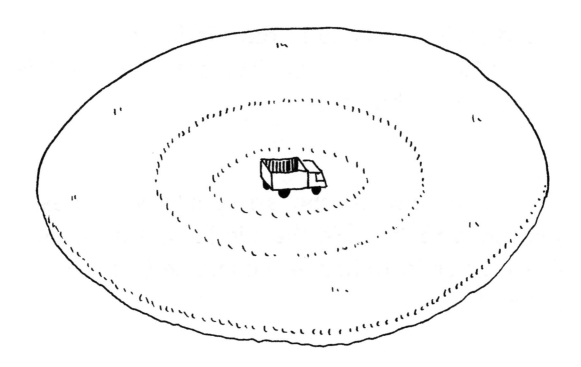

Middle

Ideas for Home

Play the tapping the beat game

Key Stage 2 Session 13: Tapping the beat

Date:............

Sit on the floor with your child opposite you. Say, 'We are going to play a clapping game, I'm Mum or Mummy.' As you say 'Mum' clap one beat and as you say 'Mummy' clap two beats.

Do the same with your child's name:

'You are George' (You clap one beat)
'You are David' (You clap two beats)
Or
'You are Samantha' (You clap three beats)

Talk about how many claps:

'Mum is one clap'
'Mummy is two claps'
'Samantha is three claps'

Think of other names of family and friends and clap them together.

Next time
Continue as above and then try to bring in other words such as 'book' (one clap), 'apple' (two claps), 'dinosaur' (three claps), 'television' (four claps).

Spend time in the week playing this game when you can. When your child is used to playing this game you won't need to sit down every time; you can play it anywhere, at any time.

Date	☺ Comment

49

George

Da   vid

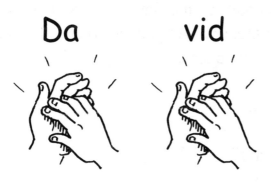

Sam   anth   a

Tapping the **beat**

Ideas for Home

More beat tapping: guess the object game

Key Stage 2 Session 14: beat tapping and guessing

Date:............

When your child is able to clap the beat to names and simple objects, go on to play this game.

Put out three things in front of your child; for example, a cup, shampoo, telephone.

Say, 'I'm going to think of one of these things and clap it and see if you can guess which one I'm thinking of.' Choose one (e.g. shampoo) and clap it. Don't say the word. Help your child to guess which word it was.

Choose each thing in turn and do this again. Praise your child for guessing. If they get it wrong, repeat the claps and say, 'Have another think.' At different times use another three objects. When your child is finding this easy, let them have a turn clapping a word for you to guess.

FORK	TEDDY	DINOSAUR
PLATE	PAPER	CHOCOLATE
BRICK	CRAYON	UMBRELLA
SHOE	GLASSES	WELLINGTON

Date	☺ Comment

Beat tapping

Ideas for Home

Storylines

Key Stage 2 Session 15: Making stories

Date:............

Choose a soft toy or character. Tell your child you are going to make a story about what the toy will do.

For example:

Teddy was sleeping under the table.
He woke up
and jumped on the sofa.
He read a book while he waited for tea.

Tell this story with actions.

Encourage your child to tell a similar simple story with the same toy. This might be:

Teddy went to ???? with ???? They saw ???? They came home and had ???? for tea.

Each time try to expand on these little stories to get more ideas and activities. Encourage your child to use action words.

Date	☺ Comment

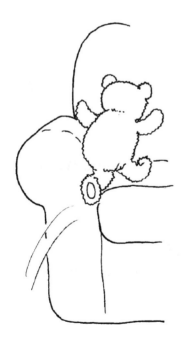

Making stories

Ideas for Home

Listen, remember and do games

Key Stage 2 Session 16: Listening, remembering and doing

Date:............

Give your child some instructions in two parts.

For example:
'We're going to play a game together – I'm going to *touch the chair* then *run to the window.'*
Then say, 'Mmm, can I remember to do two things? Let's see, let's do it together.'

Hold hands and stand still and say, 'We're going to touch the chair then run to the window.' Then say **'Go'**, and do the actions together.

Repeat these little games using simple two-part actions.
Examples could be:
'Touch your head and then walk slowly to the sofa. **Go!**'
'Jump two times then sit on the floor. **Go!**'

Do the actions together to begin with, then let the child do more on their own. Encourage the child to listen and do every bit of the action; for example, 'Walk *slowly*', 'Jump *two* times.'
If your child finds it difficult, encourage them to repeat the words of the instructions out loud to help them remember.

As your child gets used to this game you can play it anywhere – in the garden, in the park, on the way to school.
You can encourage your child to give
you two actions to do.

Praise your child for good listening and remembering.

Date	☺ Comment

Ideas for Home

Sequencing life events

Key Stage 2 Session 17: Remembering and telling

Date:.............

Sit with your child and recall what they have done today.

Get them to close their eyes and remember. Don't prompt; just give time to think and recall events of the day in sequence.

For example, the child may have got up, had breakfast, gone to school, come home, visited granny or perhaps brought a friend home.

Then ask, What did you do first? And then? And next? And after that?

Use your fingers to relate the events first and then second, and then third, and so on.

Then encourage the child to tell you these events as a 'story' using your fingers to help remember.

Praise your child for good remembering and telling.

Do this several times a week.

Date	☺ Comment

Ideas for Home

The question game: When?

Date:............

During the week play the 'When' game.

Ask your child a 'when' question.

For example, 'When do we eat breakfast?' Pause and give the answer for this: 'In the morning.'

Then, 'When do we all go to sleep?' Give the answer, 'At night time.'

Then, 'When does Susie come to visit?' 'On Tuesdays.' Then ask as many 'when' questions as you can, and encourage your child to give you an answer.

Date	☺ Comment

When?

Ideas for Home

Exploring feeling words

Key Stage 2 Session 19: Understanding the word <u>worried</u>

Date:............

Choose a soft toy animal or hand puppet. Tell a simple story about the animal feeling worried about something in the playground:

This is Adrian Bear and he came back from school and was very quiet. He sat in a chair and hid his head.
Mummy Bear said, 'Are you sad?'
He shook his head and said, 'No.'
'Are you angry?'
He shook his head and said, 'No, I'm not angry.'
'What is it then?'
'I'm worried.'
'What are you worried about, Adrian Bear?'
'I'm worried about remembering to take my friend's birthday card to school tomorrow. I may forget it.'
Mummy Bear said, 'It's good you want to remember.'

With your child, think of ideas to help Adrian Bear remember to take the card to school in the morning, e.g.

 Put it in the bag tonight

 Draw a picture and put it by the door

 Put the card by the front door where you'll see it.

Talk with your child about things that people might worry about, e.g.

 missing the bus

 forgetting something for school

 being late

 giving a wrong answer to the teacher.

Date	😊 Comment

Worried

Ideas for Home

Rhyming word games

Key Stage 2 Session 20: Using rhyming words

Date:............

Say, 'Some words end with the same sound, they rhyme; for example, toes/nose' (point as you say the word).

There are other words such as chair/hair, hat/mat, look/book, egg/peg, tree/knee, floor/door, mouse/house.

Try to find other words that rhyme.

'If you say a word (such as table) can you find or make up a word that rhymes with it – such as Mabel, cable, smable?' (Point out which ones are fun-nonsense words you made up.)

During the week, talk about words that rhyme.

Date	☺ Comment

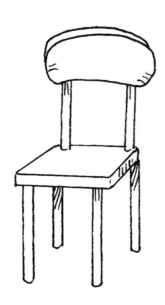

Rhyming words

Ideas for Home

Play the story game

Key Stage 2 Session 21: Telling a story

Date:............

Tell as simply as you can the story of Goldilocks and the Three Bears using mime.

Mime 'knocking on the door'	Goldilocks knocked on the door of the three bears' house. No one was in.
Mime 'eating'	She went in and ate their breakfast. She sat in a small chair and it broke.
Mime 'sleep'	She went upstairs and fell asleep. The bears came home and asked, 'Who's been eating my porridge?' 'Who's broken my chair?' 'Who's been sleeping in my bed?' And Goldilocks woke up and jumped up and ran away.

Say, 'Can you tell the story with all the actions?'

Help out with the actions if your child forgets the story, and give lots of praise. See if your child can repeat the story several days later.

Date	☺ Comment

63

Telling a story

Ideas for Home

The word pair game

Key Stage 2 Session 22: Finding rhyming pairs

Date:............

Say, 'We're going to play a game and you will need to listen really carefully. I'll say two words.
Sometimes the words will rhyme.
Sometimes the words won't rhyme (shake your head).

You can start by sitting down. If the two words rhyme, you stay sitting down.

If the two words don't rhyme, you stand up straight away. Sit down again when you hear two words that rhyme.

Some pairs of words:

Rhyme	*Don't rhyme*
cat/hat	pen/box
socks/rocks	big/little
bin/tin	home/mouse
mug/bug	cup/saucer
parrot/carrot	horse/dog

Play this game as often as you can during the week.

Date	☺ Comment

Ideas for Home

Now you tell me a story

Key Stage 2 Session 23: Retelling a story

Date:............

Say you are going to tell a story about Jack and the Beanstalk (with actions).

	Jack and his mother had to sell their cow to get some money for food. But Jack sold the cow for some magic beans instead of money.
Mime 'Jack's mum throwing the beans away'	Jack's mum was so angry that she threw the beans out of the window.
Mime 'sleeping'	While they were asleep in the night, the beans grew into a big beanstalk.
Mime 'climbing'	Jack climbed up the beanstalk and found a giant guarding some treasure.
Mime 'creeping'	He crept up and took the treasure.
Mime 'chasing'	The giant chased Jack down the beanstalk. Jack got away.

Ask the child to retell the story.

Date	☺ Comment

66

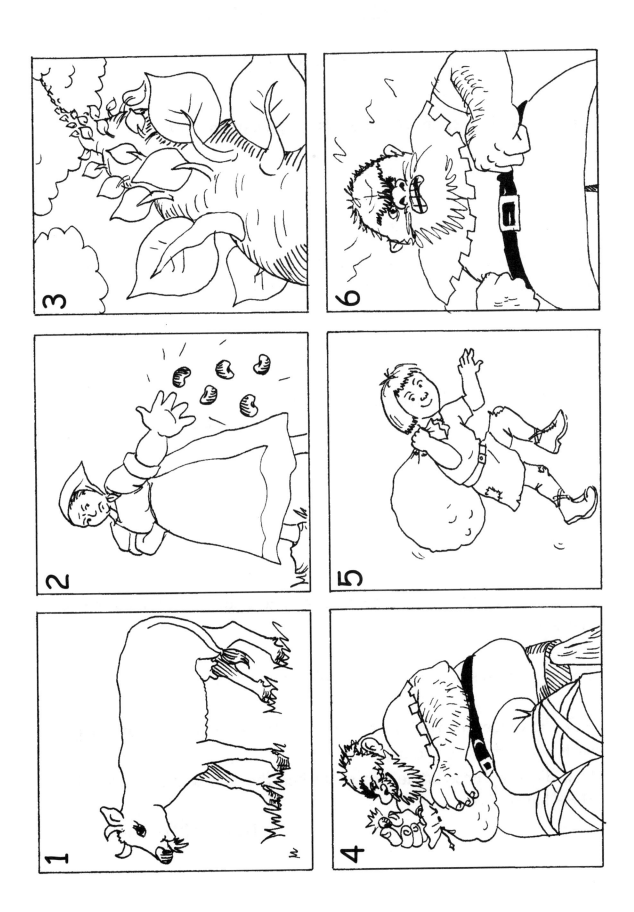

Ideas for Home

Exploring feelings

Key Stage 2 Session 24: explaining <u>feelings</u> in a story

Date:............

Tell the story about Jack and the Beanstalk

How did the mum *feel* when Jack came home and told her that he had swapped the cow for beans and not money?

Ideas

> Angry, cross?
> Worried about buying food?
> Sad because she had had the cow a long time?

How did she feel when Jack climbed up the beanstalk?

> Worried?
> Excited?

How did the giant feel when he woke up and saw Jack taking the treasure?

Spend time talking about how people feel in stories.

How did Cinderella feel when she was left behind instead of going with her sisters to the ball?
How did the Three Little Pigs feel when the wolf was trying to blow their house down?

Date	☺ Comment

Record sheet: Early Years/Nursery

Session 1   Play the hiding **under** game

Session 2   Play the **listening** game

Session 3   Play the moving **over** game

Session 4   Play the standing **on** game

Session 5   Play the **big** and **little** game

Session 6   Play the **under** game

Session 7   Play the **up** and **down** game

Session 8   Play the **on** and **under** game

Session 9   Play another **listening** game

Session 10   Play the **listen** and **do** game

Session 11   Play the **making different sounds** game

Session 12   Play the **top** and **bottom** game

Record Sheet:
Foundation/Key Stage 1

Session 1   Play the **taking turns** game   ☐ ☐ ☐

Session 2   Play the **happy** and **sad** game   ☐ ☐ ☐

Session 3   Play the **rhyming words** game   ☐ ☐ ☐

Session 4   Play the hiding game **behind**   ☐ ☐ ☐

Session 5   Play the hiding game **in front**   ☐ ☐ ☐

Session 6   Play the hiding game: **behind** and **in front**   ☐ ☐ ☐

Session 7   Play the **sounds** and **words** game   ☐ ☐ ☐

Session 8   Play the question game: **Who?**   ☐ ☐ ☐

Session 9   Play the **middle** game   ☐ ☐ ☐

Session 10   Play the question game: **Where?**   ☐ ☐ ☐

Session 11   Exploring **feeling words**   ☐ ☐ ☐

Session 12   More **middle** games   ☐ ☐ ☐

Record Sheet: Key Stage 2

Session 13	Tapping the **beat** game		
Session 14	More **beat tapping**: guess the object game		
Session 15	**Storylines**		
Session 16	**Listen, remember** and **do** games		
Session 17	Sequencing life events		
Session 18	Play the question game: **When?**		
Session 19	Exploring **feeling words**: worried		
Session 20	Play the rhyming word games		
Session 21	Play the **story** game		
Session 22	Play the **word pair** game		
Session 23	Now you tell me a **story**		
Session 24	Exploring **feelings**		

Songs and Rhymes

Incy Wincy Spider climbed up the water spout,
Down came the rain and washed poor Incy out.
Out came the sunshine and dried up all the rain,
So Incy Wincy Spider climbed up the spout again.

One, two, buckle my shoe,
Three, four, knock on the door,
Five, six, pick up sticks,
Seven, eight, lay them straight,
Nine, ten, a big fat hen.

One, two, three, four, five,
Once I caught a fish alive.
Six, seven, eight, nine, ten,
Then I let it go again.

Hickory dickory dock,
The mouse ran up the clock.
The clock struck one, the mouse ran down.
Hickory, dickory, dock.

This old man, he played one,
He played nick-nack on my drum.

Chorus
Nick-nack, paddy-whack,
Give a dog a bone,
This old man came rolling home.

This old man, he played two,
He played nick-nack on my shoe.

This old man, he played three,
He played nick-nack on my knee.

This old man, he played four,
He played nick-nack on my door.

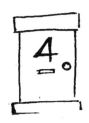

This old man, he played five,
He played nick-nack on my hive.

This old man, he played six,
He played nick-nack on my sticks.

This old man, he played seven,
He played nick-nack up in heaven.

This old man, he played eight,
He played nick-nack on my gate.

This old man, he played nine,
He played nick-nack on my spine.

This old man, he played ten,
He played nick-nack once again.

Photographer: Simon Armstrong

MAKEUP IS ART

CREATIVE MAKEUP BY AOFM

"*Dedicated to my loving Grandmother Mavis Kenneally.*
Without you this would have not been possible."

Jana

Creative Directors

Jana Ririnui & Lan Nguyen

Copy Editor
Sarah-Jane Corfield-Smith

Make up
Lan Nguyen, Jana Ririnui, Sandra Cooke, Rachel Wood, Jose Bass, Jo Sugar, Lina
Dahlbeck, Philippe Milleto, Christina Iravedra, Carolyn Roper

Writers
Jana Ririnui, Lan Nguyen, Sandra Cooke, Rachel Wood, Jo Sugar, Barbra Villasenor,
Lina Dahlbeck, Jose Bass, Sarah-Jane Corfield-Smith, Yvonne Chung, Carolyn Roper

Photographers
Camille Sanson, Catherine Harbour, Fabrice Lachant, Keith Clouston, Jason Ell,
Desmond Murray, Conrad Atton, Zoe Barling, Mo Saito,
Han Lee de Boer, Allan Chiu, Roberto Aguliar, Daniel Nadel

Hair Stylists
Jana Ririnui, Marc Eastlake, Desmond Murray, Zoe Irwin, Andrea Cassolari, Nathalie
Malbert, Natasha Mygdal, Cyndia Harvey, Fabio Vivan

Stylists
Karl Willett, Shyla Hassan, Nasrin Jean-Batiste, Svetlana Prodanic, David Hawkins,
Sampson Sobage

Front Cover by Camille Sanson @ Disciple
Makeup by Lan Nguyen, Jewellery by Loius Mariette Design by Disciple Productions
Published by AOFM 2009

ISBN 978-0-9561858-0-8

Printed and bound in the UK

Contents

Introduction 2

Skincare 5

Dermalogica 6

The Face 8

Primers 10

Foundation 12

Eyebrows 14

Eyes 16

Eyelashes 26

Highlighting 34

Blush and Contour 36

Powders 38

Bronzers 42

Lips 44

Men 54

Iconic Eras 62

Red Carpet 74

Editorial 76

Beauty Editorial 96

Advertising 100

Conceptual 105

Body Art 120

Underwater 126

Adornment 130

Tools 138

Catwalk and Backstage 143

Questions and Answers 146

Afterword 149

JANA Ririnui

Jana, Make-up artist and founder of AOFM

"I was born in New Zealand in a small town called Invercargill, far away from the fast pace of a fashion capital like London. I started my career at 14, working for free at a hair salon after school. My dream was to become a hairdresser and I was prepared to work hard to make this a reality. I moved to Australia where there were more opportunities, allowing me to build up my hairdressing skills. It was here that I was spotted and approached by a modelling agency and started to model. Although it took me away from my hairdressing, modelling gave me a wider perspective of the fashion world and experience on the other side of the camera. It was here that I realised that make-up artistry is where my heart belonged. I decided to move to London in 1999, knowing it would be the perfect place to combine my skills as a hairdresser with my potential as a make-up artist.

I studied at one of London's well known schools but upon completion of my courses as a make-up student, I felt a little lost as no-one had really prepared me for the hard road ahead or how competitive the industry was going to be. Despite the lack of guidance I worked really hard on my career and after painstaking work and testing with photographers I eventually found my feet as a make up-artist. Looking back. I took every opportunity to work - as long as I was applying make-up, I was happy. I worked on cosmetic counters, shooting on my days off with photographers and assisting for free just to gain more experience. I don't think I really began to learn about the industry until I started assisting other make-up artists. This all helped lead me to become a successful artist. I have worked on a number of famous magazines along with some big names but my passion has always been the desire to teach and provide help to aspiring make-up artists who were in the same situation as me when I finished my training.

While talking to friends and fellow make-up artists about setting up a school, it was felt there was a need to offer training conducted by professional working make-up artists.

As the industry is so small and competitive it seemed clear to us that the best people to teach make-up skills and industry know-how are those who are already successful artists themselves. I didn't get to learn about the industry until I was undertaking jobs, so I wanted to ensure my students would have the opportunity to understand the workings of the profession whilst developing their skills.

So the Academy was born. The first in the industry owned and operated by freelance make-up artists with a love of the industry. My desire is to encourage the next generation of make-up artists, giving them the tools, knowledge and understanding that is essential to succeed in the industry. My philosophy has seen AOFM's reputation grow as one of the leading make-up schools and our students have gone on to become some of the finest and successful international freelance make-up artists, as well as top fashion and beauty editors for major fashion magazines and newspapers.

I formed the AOFM Pro team which has become a well known creative force within the industry, driven by the team's flair and conceptual ideas. We have come together with other top industry professionals to create a book dedicated to inspire other make-up artists, people wishing to enter this exciting career and anyone who appreciates fine art and beauty.

This book is packed full of creative ideas, inside knowledge from our artists' experiences and advice on how this forever changing industry operates. It will keep you one step ahead of the competition and give you a true insight into the creative world of make-up artistry.

Lan Nguyen, Make-up Artist and Creative Director

LAN Nguyen

"MAKEUP is ART." This is the true definition of how I see make-up. Every face is a blank canvas and every brush stroke creates something magical. Applying make-up is an art form in itself, but the finished piece is what excites me. My inspiration comes from past and present art, from people and colours and the cosmetic products available around me. I love make-up and consider it a very important tool to help not only enhance your own natural beauty, but to build confidence for everyday life. When you feel good, you look good, and make-up helps you achieve this positive feeling.

Painting has always been a part of my life. From an early age it was all I did, poster competitions, portraits, landscape watercolour paintings. Even though I was advised to do something more mainstream as a career I refused and followed my heart which was art, where I knew at least I would be happy. I used every art medium available at the time and just wanted to create, whether it was on canvas, paper, clothes, walls or doors! Every blank space was my canvas.

I studied art and fashion design at Central Saint Martins College of Art & Design and it was here that I began my journey into the fashion industry. At college, I learned the disciplines of concept, design, creating and working with materials around me, which has been a philosophy I still apply to my work as a make-up artist today. It was during this time that I discovered that working as a make-up artist could be a successful profession.

While working as a runner at a photography studio, I was handed a set of make-up brushes and asked to help out on a busy shoot, which turned out to be not only a success, but a major turning point my life. With no experience in the make-up field, I simply treated my model like a painting and did what I thought was best.

Working and learning on the job was my form of training and I took every opportunity to experiment and develop my skills as a professional make-up artist. I networked with other make-up artists, stylists and photographers and this led me to my first collaboration on a professional high-fashion test shoot for my portfolio.

Afterwards, I was invited to assist a fashion and news photographer whom I'd met by chance. This chance meeting took me to New York, London, Milan and Paris fashion weeks. The whole experience inspired me to embrace the business of becoming a make-up artist seriously.

Seeing it all happen before my eyes was an amazing process, and gave me the drive and realisation that this was what I wanted to do. I questioned some of the top make-up artists at the shows who gave me sound advice.

I had gained invaluable knowledge by working back stage, interviewing models and dealing with picture editors from around the world and by simply being steeped in the whole process and industry. Words cannot describe the magic that happens when everyone is working under pressure as a team to produce a beautiful show.

As a make-up artist, I am always learning on the job. I get given a lot of freedom, which allows me to develop different techniques and create what I like. Some of my ideas are accidental, which have then developed into exciting projects. There is so much creativity around us and by producing this book I have only touched on one of many visions.

It has been a great pleasure collaborating with my fellow models, make-up artists, hair stylists, fashion stylists, designers, photographers and agents, especially the Academy of Freelance Make Up. Without their support I would not have been able to achieve what I have accomplished so far. For this I would like to say a personal thank you to all.

3

Photographer: Catherine Harbour
Make-up: Lan Nguyen using Lancome
Model: Kasia Z @ First Management

SKIN*Care*

As a make-up artist, it helps to understand skin, as it is the canvas that you work on. If you prepare and look after the skin well, then your make-up will sit better and last longer. It is fully recommended to study the skin to the level of a beautician, as this will help you understand the make-up application more fully.

It is not necessary to carry a skin care range for each skin type in your make-up kit. However, it is important to be able to manage and control each skin type to your advantage. Many tutors at AOFM and make-up artists are big fans of Dermalogica. It is a brand that acknowledges the importance of skin and creates products that make the make-up artist's job easier, as well as offering ongoing training for make-up artists lucky enough to be included on their artist list. The following will guide you through the essential products for a make-up artist to carry in their kit.

When choosing a skin care range, opt for one that is not highly perfumed and is suitable for use on sensitive skin. Models have make-up applied and removed so frequently that their skin becomes easily sensitised. It is also important to carry a good-quality range if you plan to work with celebrities – which is why for so many make-up artists, Dermalogica ticks the boxes.

It is important to pay attention to dry and oily skin. Dry skin needs oil and moisture put back into it, so skin preparation and products containing oil and moisture will help the make-up last longer. If you do not treat dry skin you may experience flaking, which will ruin your foundation. Oily skin needs products that help reduce shine and oil. Skin care and make-up products containing oil will cause your make-up to slide, and shine will be visible very quickly making the make-up difficult to manage.

When doing pre-recorded TV, videos, bridal make-up, beauty and fashion shoots and celebrity make-up, always use a full range of products unless the celebrity requests using their own preferred brand. Live TV or shooting on location often requires wipes and moisturiser to save time. On fashion shows, if time allows, use a full range but when pushed for time it is essential to carry wipes.

MAKEUP IS ART

Dermalogica

Cleanse

– Ultra calming cleanser is an effective and gentle cleanser that is mild enough to be used to remove eye make-up. Is also convenient on location as can be removed without water. Face wipes, such as MAC and Simple, can be used instead of cleanser and toner for speed and convenience. These are commonly used backstage and on photoshoots to remove make-up quickly and efficiently.

Tone

– Multi Active Toner is a convenient spray toner that is gentle, moisturising and refreshing. It helps prepare the skin for moisturiser, and does not need to be removed.

Exfoliate (optional)

– Daily Microfoliant is a fine powder, which when mixed with water becomes a paste that gently exfoliates the skin. Use to smooth out dry, flaky skin and remove dead skin cells. Can be removed with warm water or damp cotton wool pads.

Treat Eyes and Lips

– Multi Vitamin Power Firm contains silicone, which acts like a primer, smoothing wrinkles and moisturising the sensitive skin around the eyes and lips. Lucas paw paw ointment is great to use on dry chapped lips.

Treat the problem (optional)

– Some skins may require additional treatment for problem areas. For dry skin or to add moisture use Skin Hydrating Booster. This can also be used on the lips. For sensitive skin use Gentle Soothing Booster, which is great for reducing redness and to calm the skin. For mature skin or premature ageing, Extra Firming Booster can be used to reduce the appearance of fine lines and wrinkles. For skin prone to breakouts and spots, Special Clearing Booster is effective to help reduce breakouts.

Moisturise

– Dependant on skin type. For normal to dry skin, Skin Smoothing Cream is ideal to hydrate and smooth the skin. For oily skin, Active Moist provides a light hydration, helps reduce the appearance of oil and helps close the pores.

Even out skin tone

– Sheer Tint Moisturiser is used to moisturise the skin as well as provide sheer coverage to help even out skin tone. Ideal for people that don't want to wear a foundation but still want a little coverage.

ultracalming
cleanser

dermalogica®

a system researched and developed by The International Dermal Institute

for face
and eyes

clearing
mattifier

dermalogica®

researched and developed by The International Dermal Institute

medBac clearing™

13 FL OZ / 40 ml e

dermalogica®

mal Institute

make-up

dermal

sheer tint

moisture

SPF15

dermalogica®

a skin care system researched and developed by The International Dermal Institute

skin
hydrating
booster

extra
firming
booster

dermalogica®

developed by The International Dermal Institute

1 FL OZ /
30 mL e

special
clearing
booster

dermalogica®

medBac clearing

1 FL OZ / 30 ml e

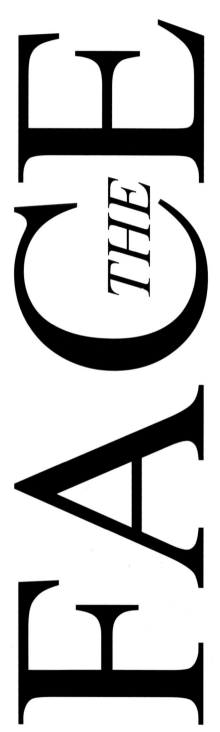

THE FACE

In today's society, how you look matters, because when you look at yourself, it reflects how you feel. Skin, make-up, hair and nails are all areas that need attention when creating the perfect look for your client. It is important for an artist to be able to cover these skills confidently, even if there are specialists available. It also helps keep the job diverse and interesting.

Cosmetic products are constantly changing. New products become available and existing ones are improved. It is important to know the ingredients and to be guided by the specialist suppliers. It is also beneficial to test the products first in case a model has become sensitive or allergic to a product. It will save you time and avoid costly mistakes.

The freedom of style, that is so prevalent now, allows us to experiment mixing the classic with the new, and by adding your own signature twist it gives it an edge. Trends always get repeated but as products change they can produce a completely different look.

There are so many timeless beauty icons to refer to but the important rule is that you enhance features to make the model look beautiful. For example, by having a beautiful base and then just a touch of colour you can create something that is fun and strong but still beautiful.

8

Photographer: Jason Ell
Make-up: Jose Base using Shu Uemura
Hair: Natasha Mygdal using Bumble & Bumble
Model: Hannah @ Next

Primers

A primer is a product used to prepare the skin before foundation, and for the most part are all silicon based. The silicon in the product is used to fill in pores and fine lines, to create a smooth base for the foundation or other make-up to be applied. The main benefit of using a primer is that it helps the make-up last longer on the skin.

There are many types of primers available, in the same way that there are numerous moisturisers for different skin types. Primers work best on cleansed, prepared skin, and, if the skin is exceptionally dry, then a primer can be used on the skin after moisturiser.

Types of primers include hydrating primers used for moisturising dry skin, mattifying primers for oily skin used to help control shine, and primers to plump the skin for a more youthful appearance. Many primers also contain a SPF. Primers can come in a range of textures, such as lotions, mousse, silicon gels as well as mineral powder primers (for sensitive skin).

Professional make-up artists, particularly those in the fashion industry, tend to have a range of different primers in their kits for use on different jobs. Although in the fashion industry we generally look after models with young, plump skin, and are able to be on set to do touch-ups in between shots, there are still occasions when primers are needed, such as shooting an outdoor editorial where a primer with SPF is essential. Models with tired or dehydrated skin (we see this a lot during fashion week) may require a hydrating primer to help sooth and smooth the skin.

Primers are more popular in the TV and film industry, where a range of different aged actors and presenters are used. In addition, being on set or on location and under warm lights for long periods of time requires make-up to last longer in between touch-ups by the make-up artist.

With the growing industry of high-definition TV and film, the amount of make-up worn by actors and presenters needs to be more natural and yet still effective. As powders can look heavy on TV and film, mattifying primers are ideal to help prevent shine and reduce the need for excess powder and continual touch-ups. In addition, on the more mature actors and presenters, a silicon-based primer, such as produced by MAC, will help smooth over fine lines to form a stmooth base for foundation to go more flawlessly on skin. The Becca Line and Pore Corrector is a skin tone oil-free primer, which can help minimize the pores and lines around the eyes and nose for a smoother base application.

Photographer: Keith Clouston
Hair & Make-up: Jana Ririnui using Becca
Model: Yu @ Oxygen

MAKEUP IS ART

Foundation

Foundation and Concealers

The main point of using a foundation or base is to even out the tone and colour of the skin. How a make-up artist wants the skin to appear varies from job to job. Of course all creative briefs differ On one project a make-up artist may want the skin to have a glow, while on other jobs, an old-fashioned matte, full coverage base may be needed or the make-up artist may also be required to create a natural-looking finish, as if there is no foundation applied at all.

Choosing what type of product to use is one of the biggest challenges a new make-up artist can face. Here is a guide to help sort out the confusion:

Full Coverage

Gives skin the appearance of flawlessness. A good full coverage can effectively cover scars, discolouration and blemishes - almost like a concealer - for the entire face. These foundations also work well on Asian and black skin tones.

* *Tip* - to get a flawless base on any skin type, dilute the full coverage or stick by mixing it with a sheer fluid tinted moisturiser.

* Recommended products - Bobbi Brown Foundation Stick; Becca Foundation Stick; MAC Full Coverage Foundation, a water-resistant formula

Sheer Coverage

Lets the skin look natural and unmade. Will even out skin tone, but allows freckles, beauty marks etc to be visible, giving the effect of make-up-free.

* Recommended product – MAC Face And Body Foundation, a water-based and water-resistant formula, this is often used to even out the skin all over the body

Oil Free/Oil Control

Great for those with oily skin and can help keep shine at bay creating a matte-textured finish. Usually, oil free means no lanolin or mineral oils (those are the oils that tend to clog pores and cause sensitivity).

* Recommended product - Nars Oil Free Foundation, a liquid formula that gives a lovely medium coverage with a natural matte finish

Illuminating

A foundation that leaves the skin with a glow and luminous finish. Some illuminating foundations can have small pearl and glitter particles in it. When working on photo shoots, this can make the skin look greasy.

* Recommended products – Chanel Vitalumière Foundation; Giorgio Armani Foundation

Moisturising

A base best used on dry to normal skin type. It gives extra hydration and works well on mature skin.

* Recommended product – Bobbi Brown Luminous Moisturising Foundation

Cream to Powder

Has a more traditional, old-fashioned texture. Usually packaged in a compact, it goes on creamy but dries to a powder finish. Gives a medium finish and is great for skin that wants a touch more coverage than a liquid foundation, but not as heavy as a full coverage.

* Recommended products - Shu Uemura Nobara Cream Foundation, often used on film sets; MAC Studio Tech Foundation, gives skin a very smooth texture when photographed

Powder Based

Best used on oily skin as it has no liquid or moisture in it. Another advantage is that it can be used with a brush to set make-up. It also gives a matte non-reflective finish to the skin.

*Recommended product – MAC Studio Fix

Mousse

A whipped, textured product that gives a light coverage and a natural glow or matte finish, which feels light on the skin.

* Recommended products – Max Factor Miracle Touch Foundation; Maybelline Dream Matte Mousse Foundation; Lancôme Magie Matte Mousse Foundation

Tinted moisturiser

A combination of a moisturiser and some colour, it is perfect for evening out the skin tone. It gives a very light coverage and sinks easily into the skin.

* Recommended products – Becca Luminous Skin Colour; Laura Mercier Tinted Moisturiser, contains SPF and they do a range for oily skin, too

Concealers

Concealers are used to cover blemishes and imperfections once a foundation has been applied. They offer heavier coverage and also help cover dark circles under the eyes.

* Recommended products – Estée Lauder Maximum Cover, a lightweight full-coverage foundation often used as a concealer by make-up artists; Lancôme Rénergie Lift Makeup SPF20, has a light silicone base that helps to conceal fine lines and wrinkles; MAC Studio Finish, great for covering moles, tattoos and birthmarks, also works wonders on Asian skin tones where dark circles can be more prominent.

13

Photographer: Keith Clouston
Hair & Make-up: Jana Ririnui using Bobbi Brown
Model: Leanne @ Oxygen

MAKEUP IS ART

Eyebrows

Eyebrows are the frame of the face. Therefore, it is good to have them clean, visible, and in a shape that matches the face.

For the natural symmetrical look:

The length of the eyebrows must be slightly longer than the eye, meaning that the brow needs to start just above the tear duct and end approx 5mm after the outer corner of the eye. This will create a young and fresh look.

When it comes to the arch of the eyebrow you have to be very careful. To find the correct place to have the arch, do the following:

Look straight into a mirror, place the handle of a thin make-up brush on the outside of your nostril and point it so that it is in line with the outside of your iris. Where the brush crosses the brow is where the highest point of the arch should be.

To really define the brow, remove all the hairs on top of the eyebrow. If you are worried, imagine a straight line from the start of your eyebrow up to the highest point of the arch. All the hairs above this line are unnecessary so pluck them away. This will leave you with a sharp and defined brow shape.

Repeat the same process underneath the brow. Imagine a straight line from beneath to the highest point of the arch, everything under this line can be taken away. Be very careful as you pluck as three hairs plucked away or kept can make a huge difference.

Another way of shaping the eyebrows is to trim them. Where there is excess hair, or for any hairs that are particularly unruly, brush them upwards and trim off any length that goes over the imaginary lines mentioned in the previous steps.

If your brows still need more definition then you can apply a little brow shadow to outline the new defined shape. Use an ashy brown on lighter brows and for really dark brows you can try a plum tone.

If you want a cat-ish brow look, then make them longer and straighter. This is a great look for older women who want to look a little younger.

If you want to disguise your own brow and draw a completely new one then a great tip is to wet some soap, apply it like a paste over the eyebrow and then carefully add a good concealer on top. You can then draw any style of eyebrow that you want.

The best way to get really good at styling eyebrows is to practice on paper. Try drawing different styles and shapes. Avoid having your arch in the middle of the brow. It will make the eyes look narrow. By having the arch a little further along, the eyes will look open and full.

Don't pluck the start of the brow too much, if the brows look too far apart from each other it will make the eyes look like they are on the side of the head - like a fish!

The best tweezers have pointy ends and can only take one hair out at a time. Tweezers with a slanted edge will take lots of hairs out in one go, which can lead to over-plucking, resulting in the wrong shape brow.

14

Photographer: Allan Chiu
Make-up: Jose Bass using Shu Uemura
Model: Anna @ FM

EYES

16

EYES * LASHES * TOOLS

Photographer: Roberto Aguliar
Make-up: Jose Bass using Shu Uemura

Eye Shadow Textures

Eye shadow
How the colour of the eye shadow appears on the eyelid depends on the cosmetic brand used, its texture and its application. Using an eye primer or eye shadow base, such as Benefit's Lemon Aid, can boost an eye shadow's appearance on the eyelid and make the make-up on the eye area lasting longer.

Matte
Matte eye shadow is a flat colour without shine. It's a great choice as a contour or crease colour on a photo shoot as it gives a better appearance of depth. A contour eye shadow brush is a very useful tool to get this desired effect.

Cream
Cream shadows have a moist or wet texture. Some cream shadows that stay moist appear wet on the lid but are prone to creasing. Some cream eye shadows go on wet, but set and dry. Bobbi Brown's Long-wear Cream Shadow has a great crease-proof formula when set on the lid. Cream shadows also work well as a base on the eyelid to intensify the colour of a powder shadow.

Frost
A frost eye shadow will have a crystal-like shine to the finish. When applying a frost to the eyelid, choose a stiff brush over a fluffy type eye shadow brush, which will give a stronger application of the frosted pigment.

Glitter
A glitter eye shadow will contain small particles of sparkle to reflect light. Glitter eye shadows are a favourite choice of make-up artists working on music videos, pop promos and night shoots as they add a real wow factor. Loose glitter can be applied on the eye like a shadow, but need a sticky surface for it to grip onto, such as a cream shadow or eyelash glue.

Loose pigment
A loose-pigmented eye shadow is made up of tiny particles of colour and usually comes in a small pot with a lid rather than a flat casing. You can get varying degrees of effects with loose pigment shadow. If applied to the eye area with a fluffy brush, it usually creates a sheer wash of colour. If loose pigment is applied to the eyelid with a tool that is denser, such as a basic eye shadow pad, then you get a more non-transparent and stronger tone. Loose pigment eye shadow can also be mixed into a liquid, such as MAC's Mixing Medium to create a liquid make-up that can be painted onto the skin. Barry M's range of loose eye shadow pigments come in a terrific colour palette.

18

Photographer: Fabrice Lachant
Make-up: Sandra Cooke using MAC
Hair: Nathalie Malbert
Model: Olena @ Nevs

Photographer: Keith Clouston
Hair & Make-up: Jana Ririnui using Illamasqua
Model: Leanne @ Oxygen

MAKEUP IS ART

Photographer: Daniel Nadel
Make-up: Jo Sugar using Mac
Model: Sophie Willing

22

Photographer: Camille Sanson
Make-up: Lan Nguyen using Bobbi Brown
Hair: Andrea Cassolori
Model: Hannah @ Next

Eyeliners

The pencil is one of the most popular forms of eyeliner. They are generally the easiest to apply and, when sharpened, produce a nice clean line and any mistakes are easy to correct. A common trend with make-up companies today is to produce a kohl pencil with a softer lead that is gentle for use on the eye and can be smudged to create a more smoky effect.

Using a black pencil in the inner rim of the eye will make it appear smaller and more sultry.

A white pencil in the inner rim opens up the eyes, reduces the appearance of redness, and makes eyes appear more bright and alert.

There is a huge choice in pencil eyeliners, they are available in every colour of the rainbow and are available in a metallic, matte or satin finish.

Waterproof eyeliners cannot be used on the inner rim of the eyes.

Liquid eyeliners

Liquid eyeliners are a wet, almost ink-like liner, and can be applied using a brush, or often come packaged with a wand or calligraphy pen type nib. They range in sizes, so you can get very thin brushes to create fine lines or thicker wider brushes to create a more striking eyeliner effect.

Liquid eyeliners can take a minute or so to dry. Any movement while wet can create a smudge. These can be tricky to use and mistakes can be messy to correct, but once dry, your liner is set all day (or night). Liquid eyeliners tend to have a shiny finish once dry.

Gel eyeliner

As the name implies, they have a soft gel-like texture and require a brush to apply. They dry reasonably quickly, but can also be moved or smudged. When almost dry they give an eye shadow effect, but with more staying power. They are less messy than their liquid counterparts and by using a fine brush you can create really precise lines.

Cake eyeliners

Cake eyeliner is a flat pressed powder, which is used with a wet brush to create a bold line. This can intensify the lashes or smoky eye look. If the pigment is not strong enough, the eyeliner will not be as striking. A thin flat brush or angle brush is used to apply the cake eyeliners.

Make-up artists will sometimes expand on this idea, and create an eyeliner using a highly pigmented powder or eye shadow and a wet brush dipped in a mixing medium or water. This is used mainly to create a more unusual colour.

23

Photographer: Catherine Harbour
Make-up: Sandra Cooke using MAC
Hair: Nathalie Malbert
Model: Robyn @ FM

Photographer: Camille Sanson
Hair & Make-up: Cristina Iravedra using Bobbi Brown
Model: Claudia @ Nevs

EYE Lashes

Mascaras

Ask any make-up artist and they will tell you that the quality of a mascara is largely based on its wand. The trend in recent years is to go back to the old-school wands – how it was back in the 1950's. Mascaras come in a variety of formulas and colours – from the usual blacks, browns and clear, to blue, green, purple, gold, silver, white etc.

There are mascaras that claim to lengthen, thicken, curl the lashes, or a combination of the above. Some mascaras come with a primer, to help coat the lashes before the colour is applied. This is normally to thicken the lashes. Then there are the new formulations of mascara, which form tubes over individual lashes and are removed by wiping them off with water.

Mascaras are also available in a waterproof formula, although these can be harder to remove at the end of the day.

Although there are many great mascaras on the market, a good make-up artist can make most mascaras work for them using the following tips:

- Always curl the lashes

- Make sure the mascara has not dried out (mascaras have a 2-3 month shelf life after opening)

- Apply a few coats of mascara, concentrating the mascara at the base of the lashes making sure every lash has been coated, and use an eyelash comb to make sure there are no clumps

In addition to mascara for eyelashes, there are also mascaras for brows. They are used to either slightly lighten or darken the eyebrows and have a more natural effect than filling in eyebrows with powders or pencils. They usually come in colours, such as blonde, brown, dark brown and red, to match hair colours. Clear mascara is also used to comb and hold eyebrows in place.

28

Photographer: Catherine Harbour
Make-up: Lan Nguyen using Shu Uemura
Hair: Andrea Cassolari
Model: Adrienn Densi @ Nevs

Eyelashes

Eyelashes have a significant presence in the industry and can be customised by adding feathers, diamanté beads and glitter. There are so many choices available for you to be creative with.

By doubling up on lashes it can give a different dimension on the eye as they can make an eye look bigger or more sultry. Individual eyelashes are great to add on the corners or you can cut from a strip to give the eye a cat's eye look.

In a more creative way, placing them under the eye and in the sockets can give an interesting look on a shoot.

Also, by mixing pigments or glitter with clear mascara, a lash-mixing medium or clear glue, you can alter the texture, colour and shape.

There is no limit to what you can achieve.

Photographer: Camille Sanson
Make-up: Lan Nguyen using Shu Uemura
Hair: Andrea Cassolari
Stylist: Nasrin Jean-Baptiste
Model: Erin @ Nevs

MAKEUP IS ART

Photographer: Catherine Harbour
Make-up: Jana Ririnui using Shu Uemura
Model: Kasia @ First

Photographer: Fabrice Lachant
Make-up: Lan Nguyen using Shu Uemura
Hair and Skull caps: Marc Eastlake
Model: Monika R @ Next

Highlighting

Highlighting products are an essential element to help sculpt and contour the face. Where contour colours are used to create shadow and depth, highlighting products are used to reflect light, which adds an additional dimension of definition to the face. Highlighting is particularly popular in the fashion industry, in both editorial and catwalk shoots, where make-up is used to tell stories, create illusions and compliment the fashion designer's vision.

Highlighting products come in a range of different textures, from shimmer powders, cream sticks, to liquids and gels. There are different names for these products including illuminisers, shimmers, iridescent and pearlised powders, but they all do the same thing.

An illuminiser (such as the BECCA Shimmering Skin Perfector) is great mixed with a foundation to create a dewy, radiant glow and to even out skin tone. A slightly bronzed illuminiser mixed with foundation can add a subtle, bronzed, healthy glow.

Shimmer powder or liquids placed above the cheekbone reflect light and further enhance cheekbones. The YSL Touche Éclat was originally designed for use as an illuminiser, but has proved popular as a concealer for under the eye. The highlighting effect is used to reflect light and brighten dark circles.

Applying shimmer in a straight line down the centre of the nose creates the illusion of a straighter smaller nose. Highlighters can also be applied to the centre of the lips to create the illusion of plumped, fuller lips.

On the catwalks, cream shimmers are often applied to the face first, then a powder shimmer is applied on top to create a strong reflective effect. Highlighting is not just restricted to the face, but can also be used on the body to create the illusion of longer, more slender limbs. Highlighters can be brushed on to the collarbones and down the arms and the centre of the shins to give the illusion of length. Alternatively, oils can be used on the body to create a more reflective 'wet' shine. MAC strobe cream is a popular choice for highlighting the body and is used mixed in with foundations.

Photographer: Zoe Barling
Make-up: Sandra Cooke using Giorgio Armani
Hair: Natasha Mygdal using Bumble & Bumble
Model: Emma C @ IMG

Photographer: Fabrice Lachant
Make-up: Sandra Cooke using Nars
Hair: Natalie Malbert
Model: Olena @ Nevs

Blusher is the one product that can instantly make you look younger, healthier and prettier. A good blusher replaces the natural colours in your cheeks that drain away with age.

There are two types of blusher; cream and powder. Recently cosmetic brands have developed sculpting blushers that can be combined to create a strong and contoured cheekbone. Some powder blushes can be highly pigmented so you end up with excess product on the brush and it can look overdone, especially if placed too near to the nose.

For best results, the skin should be prepped and foundation applied carefully. Apply the blush onto the high apple of the cheekbones and softly blend backwards, following the cheekbone and ending at the hairline. For extra contouring and a more chiseled look, a bronzed or darker colour can be used. Mixing cream blushers and then blending with a powder blush can also look very effective and beautiful on the skin.

Black and white photography shoots require clever use of contouring and highlighting as the contrast of light and dark shadows affect the tone and shade of make-up. Cool colours will seem lighter than what they are and warm colours will appear grey and darker. Black pencil liner or eye shadow will look dark grey so a generous application is needed.

BLUSH & Contour

POWDERS

There are a few options when working with powders.

A traditional loose translucent powder, provides a sheer microfine finish, sets foundation and smoothes out skin texture caused by harsh lights. Mattes the skin and can be directly applied after moisturiser - just blot the skin prior to powder application. Gives the look of a natural skin with a perfected finish. Loose translucent powder is also used under the eye to protect the face from any fall out of shadows.

Pressed powder and loose powder serve the same purpose. I prefer to use a pressed blot powder as the packaging is compact and they designed to provide shine control without adding any noticeable colour or texture. Blot powder is great for frequent touch ups in and on set to eliminate the shine caused by the strong lights. Blot powder contains both Mica and Silica to absorb excess oils. They can be applied using a puff which will give you maximum coverage or dusted on with a brush to get a more sheer application.

Powders two shades lighter or even a white loose powder makes a great highlighter under the eyes, on the cheekbones and the highlights of the face. Keep in mind that while working on set the heat from the lighting may cause the powder to darken and eventually causing the texture of the skin to look heavy… "cakey" .

Photographer: Camille Sanson

40

Bronzers

Bronzers and Fake Tans

Being tanned or bronzed gives people that healthy glow generally associated with a nice relaxing holiday in the sun. It also gives the appearance of being slimmer and helps hide skin imperfections. However, people are now aware, more than ever, that real tans can prematurely age skin and cause skin cancer - hence the beauty industry's fascination with fake tan (not sun beds). Considering spring/summer fashion collections are shot during the winter, make-up artists have a great need for fake tans and bronzers.

On a photo shoot, make-up artists have a number of options to tan the skin. An airbrush machine can be used to apply temporary tans to models, while alcohol-based airbrush paints are great, as they don't rub off on clothes or in water. Instead, they are quick to dry, and can be easily applied with a compressor and a specialised body air gun. This however can be messy and requires specialist equipment, product and make-up remover.

To create that sun-kissed glow without an air gun, the make-up artist has a variety of different products and options. At fashion week it is common to see make-up artists using body foundation, often mixed with moisturiser, to cover blemishes and darken the legs/arms/back and any other skin showing on the models.

There are also numerous bronzing products available, such as bronzed oils, gels, lotions and creams, that all provide an instant tan, but can easily be washed off at the end of a shoot. These sorts of products are not ideal to use with certain clothes as they can stain. Make-up artists will either apply the product directly onto the skin or combine it with moisturisers. Powdered bronzers are also great, but are generally better used on smaller areas such as the face and chest, rather than the whole body. Shimmer bronzers can also be used to accentuate and highlight points such as the front of the shins, thighs, shoulders and collar bone.

For a lasting tan, the quickest and most efficient way to get that all over bronzed glow is to get a spray tan, applied by a trained therapist using a spray gun. You can choose from a light golden glow to very dark tan and the colour is dependent on the number of coats you wish to have applied. Most tans will develop over a couple of hours. Prior to the tanning, it is recommend that a full-body exfoliation is done so that all rough skin is removed – this helps the tan go on evenly. Spray tans usually last about a week, and can be maintained with proper body exfoliation and moisturising, as well as weekly top-ups.

There are other at-home fake tan options, such as aerosol sprays, creams, gels and lotions, These can be messy and can take time to dry, but do provide a good alternative to the spray tan.

The newest trend in fake tans is the gradual tan - body moisturisers with a hint of fake tan that gradually build up to create and maintain a healthy glow.

For those wishing to be bronzed for a special one-off event, there are numerous body and face bronzers that will wash off with water at the end of the night. The only downside with this option is that should it be extremely hot, or raining, your beautiful healthy glow may run off, or even worse, cause streaks! Bronzers can also tend to get on clothes, although most are water based so are easily washed off.

For make-up artists, bronzers are ideal for changing the skin tone on photo shoots, as it is quick, easy and can be applied exactly where it's needed. Again, the bronzers can come in a variety of different textures such as creams, lotions, sprays and powders.

Facial bronzers can be very simply applied all over the face or, to give that real sun-kissed glow, applied only on the places where the sun would fall, as it would if you were tanning naturally, along the cheek bones, temples, forehead and lightly along the length of the nose and the chin. This soft wash of colour will lift the face giving an extra-healthy glow.

There are so many products available now that give such a good tan effect that there is no excuse for anybody to go out and soak up the sun and burn their skin. The colour choices are vast and suit everyone from the whitest white to olive skin tones. They do require a little effort, but in the long run will save your skin and allow you to walk round with a year-long healthy glow.

43

MAKEUP IS ART

LIPS

GLOSSES * MATTS *
APPLICATION * TOOLS

Photographer: Conrad Attan
Make-up: Lan Nguyen using MAC

LIPSTICK *textures*

When choosing a lipstick (and this rule applies to most make-up) it's always best to remember that what a product looks like in it's tube is not always as it appears on the skin. This is because of the product's texture. In fashion and styling, make-up textures are as important as the colour.

If you are trying to get a truer sense of a lipstick colour, then you can neutralise the lip by using a concealer or lip primer. Lip Plump by Benefit or Lip Erase by MAC are both make-up artist favourites.

Beware of cold sores on the lip area of your model. Approach with caution as using a lip brush on an infected area and then placing that brush onto your lipstick can infect your product. Disposable hygiene lip wands like the ones from thepromakeupshop.com are essential to have in a make-up kit.

Preparing the lips

It is important to prep the lip before applying lipstick, just like you would prep the skin before applying make-up to the face. Dry, flaky or cracked lips can ruin the finished result on your lip look. You can gently exfoliate the lips by using a treatment like Hollywood Lips' Sweet Sugar Scrub then apply their Soothing Day Relief to heal and protect. Glam Balm by Rodial buffs and also plumps up the lips.

Sheer Lipstick

This is a transparent veil of colour that allows the natural lip tone to come through by creating a see-through effect. No matter how much product you apply to the lips when using a sheer tone the effect will be very limited in colour. They're not the best choice if you want to build a strong colour. Sheer lipsticks are great when you want to create a make-up look that is natural with only a hint of colour. A very popular example of a natural-looking sheer lipstick is Laura Mercier's Bare Lips, which is a pinky brown shade. A lip stain like Benefit's Benetint goes one step further as it slightly colours the lips without the look of any coating of lipstick on top of the lips.

Matt Lipstick

Matt lipstick gives a flat colour without shine or gloss and most matt lipsticks are dense in colour. They are great for more mature models as they are less likely to bleed into fine lines around the lip area. Matt lipsticks are great for creating period looks from the 1920's to the 1950's. For example, if you wanted to create a 1940's lip - a matt red like MAC Russian Red would be perfect.

Cream or Satin Lipstick

Lipsticks that are cream or satin textured have a smooth appearance with a touch of sheen that appears almost moist. Cream and satin lipsticks can have different levels of transparency depending on the brand. Cream and satin lipsticks are a great choice for bridal make-up as they have a hint of moisture, but have more colour than a sheer. Ladies Choice lipstick by Benefit is a pert-toned pink with a satin/cream texture that is great choice for brides.

Frost Lipstick

Frosted lipsticks have a touch of glimmer or metallic added to the colour to create a shimmer effect. Frosted lipsticks can also have different variation of transparency like cream or satin tones. These are a good choice if you want to create lips with reflective shine without using lip gloss. Revlon's Silver City Pink is a terrific choice for a 1960's retro lip.

Opaque Lipstick

Opaque lipstick has a dense colour and is used to fully cover the natural lips. An opaque lipstick can have a matt, satin, frost or gloss finish, but the colour is non-transparent. An example of an opaque lipstick with frost and a touch of sheen is CB96 by MAC - it's an orange lipstick that also has gold frost running through it, but the colour is full on. If you want to create lips with high colour it's best to choose one that is opaque.

Photographer: Keith Clouston
Make-up: Sandra Cooke using Illamasqua
Model: Lina O'Connor @ NEVS

Creative lips

Always block out the lips with concealer or foundation before applying lipstick to create a clean base. The colours tend to appear truer, too.

Lip liners are useful to recreate a different lip shape or to enhance the existing fullness. By colouring the whole lip you can build a solid base and then add a lipstick to intensify the colour.

Other products such as eye shadow, cream eye shadow, loose powder pigment, greasepaints, and blush creams can also be used on the lips.

Tip: Pressing the product onto the lips firmly with your finger is sometimes easier to control.

Adding gloss on top will also add volume to lips and by mixing colours you can create interesting tones.

Using shimmer or glitter on top gives high shine for photo shoots.

Photographer: Cat Harbour
Make-up: Lan Nguyen using Dior

Photographer: Fabrice Lachant
Make-up: Lan Nguyen using MAC

Photographer: Catherine Harbour
Make-up: Sandra Cooke using Illamasqua
Model: Robyn @ FM

52

Photographer: Conrad Atton
Make-up: Lan Nguyen using MAC
Model: Hannah @ Next

MEN

The cosmetic industry is no longer the sole domain of women. There has been a major shift in attitudes towards men's grooming in the last decade, which has been reflected with the growing number of cosmetic ranges designed and targeted towards men. This initially started with products for shaving, and has since expanded into skincare and make-up.

Grooming is the term commonly used to describe hair and make-up for men on a photo shoot. The art of grooming is to make the male model look fresh with clear skin and groomed hair, but without appearing to be made up. In the days of film and soft lighting, grooming was less important, but in today's high-definition environment, it is important that the male models look their 'natural' best.

In addition, the prominence of male models in the fashion industry is also increasing, with the rise of more dedicated male fashion magazines (such as GQ and Maxim), men's fashion editorial stories (featuring male models and menswear designers) and the men's fashion weeks held in Milan and Paris each season.

Grooming generally involves cleansing and moisturising the skin, correcting skin tone, concealing blemishes, reducing shine, combing the brows and shaving or plucking facial hair if required. If you're at a shoot with no stylist, then grooming also involves cutting and trimming as well as styling the hair. Grooming is not just limited to the above the neck, but also includes ensuring the hands and nails are in good shape, and that the body is well moisturised and the correct skin tone.

Increasingly though, for catwalk and editorial pieces, grooming can also include applying eye make-up such as eye shadows and eyeliners, contouring and highlighting the face, and even applying crazy paints and colours. At men's fashion weeks, there are dedicated teams of make-up artists, hair stylists and nail technicians to groom and apply make-up for the male models for the shows to mirror the visions of the designers. So, it seems that the future of grooming will no longer be grooming only, but rather the art of make-up.

Photographer: Catherine Harbour
Grooming: Lan Nguyen using Kiehls
Model: Nicholas Robinson

MAKEUP IS ART

Photographer: Fabrice Lachant
Grooming: Lan Nguyen using Lancome Homme
Stylist: Karl Willett
Model: Max @ Dynamite Hosts
Crown by Fred Butler, Underwear by CK

58

Photographer: Fabrice Lanchant
Make-up: Lan Nguyen using Mac
Styling: Karl Willett
Headpiece by Fred Butler

Photographer: Fabrice Lachant
Make-up Left: Lan Nguyen using Mac
Make-up Right: Lina Dahlbeck using MAC
Styling: Karl Willett
Models: Alex Beer and Anthony Lowther
From left to right: Skull by Butler & Wilson,
Headpiece Stylists own

ICONIC ERAS

The 1920's flapper, the 1940's brow, the 1950's Marilyn Monroe vamp, and the 1960's Twiggy, all these, and more iconic make-up styles, are used over and over in film and fashion. Every year, we see another revival. Designers take inspiration from the past, foreign cultures and street fashion and bring old trends to life with a new twist. The same goes for the make-up companies. New colours, products and techniques are brought back and re-introduced. We see brightly coloured lips all over the catwalks one season and gothic black eyes the next.

The 1920's and 1930's were all about the dark and defined with bee-sting lips and dark eyes. In recent years, we've seen this look on numerous catwalk shows, such as the looks created by Pat McGrath at Galliano for Dior. Eyebrows were kept natural and unplucked in the twenties, while eyes were dark and smoky. The incredibly beautiful actress Louise Brooks, LuLu, was one of the fashion and beauty icons of the 1920's with her trademark Dutch bob and dramatic make-up. Greta Garbo set the trend in the 1930's with plucked and drawn-in brows. The dark and smoky eyes are still one of the most popular make-up looks today.

The 1940's, the swing era or more remembered for World War II, saw women join the workforce when men were off fighting. Looks were simplified; the red lipstick became a necessity. Lips were true red with the top lip overdrawn and rounded, heavy eyeliner was flicked at the outer corners and eyebrows were kept natural.

The 1950's, also known as the glam Hollywood era, is still current and trendy and the pin-up Marilyn Monroe look has been adapted by Christina Aguilera, Scarlett Johansson and Dita Von Teese, to name just a few. Throughout this decade, there was a transformation from the ponytail and innocent teenage look to the heavily styled beehive hair and defined eyes. Starlets wore red lipstick, eyeliner, blusher, and lots of mascara. Eyebrows were kept natural and grown out. The teenagers at the time started wearing pink and peach coloured lipstick, as parents didn't approve of the heavily made-up looks.

The 1960's saw a complete change in make-up trends. Twiggy was discovered in 1966 and changed the world of fashion and beauty with her short androgynous hair-do and mod fashion, created by designers such as Mary Quant. Twiggy wore light pastel lipstick and eye shadow, false eyelashes, thick eyeliner, drawn in socket lines and lots and lots of mascara. Mary Quant is just one of many designers who take credit for inventing the miniskirt and hot pants. In the mid-sixties Mary Quant brought out a new, trendy make-up line that offered multi-use products and palettes.

The end of the sixties was the beginning of the flower-power era and women's liberation. Make-up was kept minimal and natural. Hair was left long and un-styled and not surprisingly, cosmetics companies struggled during this period.

The 1970's saw a mix of glam-rock, disco and punk music that would soon spice up and change the world of fashion and beauty. Clothes were fitted, trousers were flared and unisex looks were introduced. Make-up was bold and garish and lots of colour and glitter was used. French and Italian Vogue showed models wearing blood-red lipstick, black eye make-up and pencil thin eyebrows. David Bowie and Roxy Music were the faces of glam rock. The make-up was bold, colourful and above all, theatrical. Punk music and the anarchy movement dominated the end of the seventies' social scene; safety pins became nose and ear jewellery, hair was harshly dyed, styled and sculpted into mohawks or spikes. Vivienne Westwood and her partner Malcolm McLaren created the iconic Sex Pistols look.

The 1980's saw an explosion of colour. Big and eccentric hairstyles and make-up looks were popularised by TV, film and music stars. TV shows such as Dynasty, Miami Vice and Fame coupled with major artists like Michael Jackson and Madonna were a few of the influences. Duran Duran and Adam and the Ants were the faces of the new romantic scene and experimented with androgynous looks.

Hair was worn big and frizzy by both sexes throughout the eighties and lots of hair products were used. The mullet is the most iconic hairstyle for this era, while make-up was colourful and bold. Women wore brightly coloured mascaras and bold eye shadows blended up to the eyebrow. Blushers were also applied in excess and blended up to the hairline.

1920's

Photographer: Fabrice Lachant
Make-up: Lina Dahlbeck using Krayolon
Hair: Andrea Collaspri
Model: Emily S @ Nevs

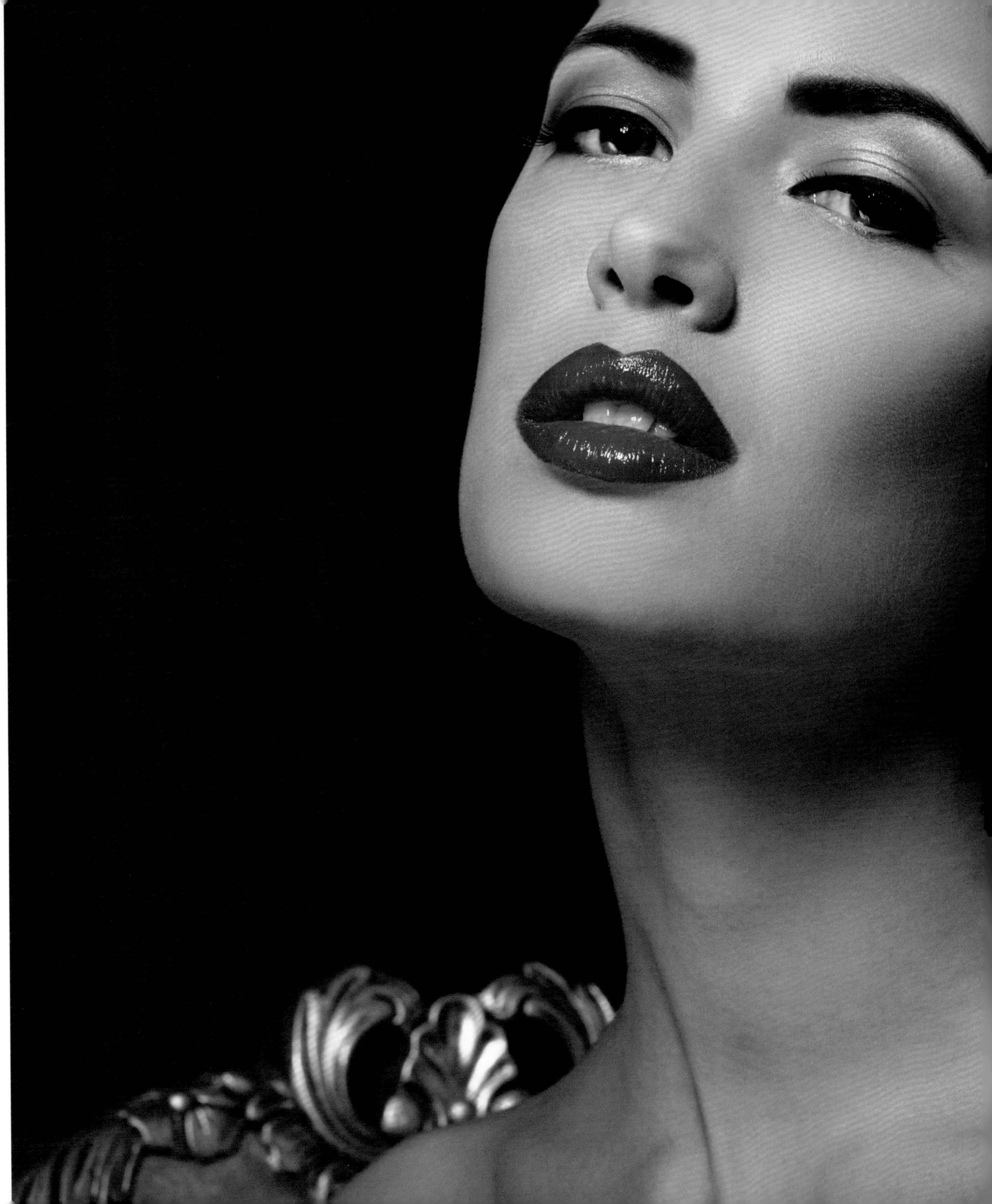

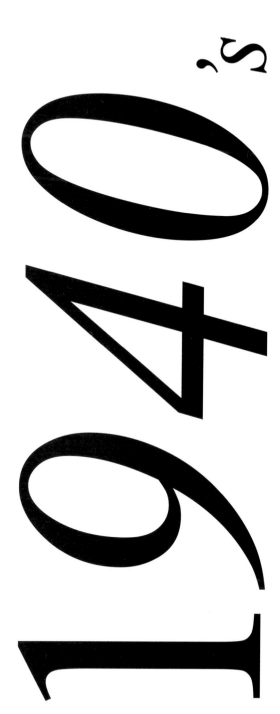

1940's

Photographer: Catherine Harbour
Make-up: Rachel Wood using Chanel
Hair: Marc Eastlake using Bumble & Bumble
Model: Sabrina @ Next

MAKEUP IS ART

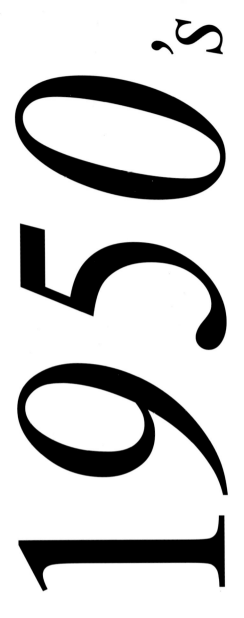

Inspired from the original Barbie-doll look mixed with I Love Lucy's Lucile Ball.

Wide eyes were painted with a powder-blue shadow, white eyeliner applied on the inside of the eye and black liquid liner - thicker in the middle of the eye - across the lid, with a touch of white loose shimmer eye shadow on the middle of the lid to create a touch of high glamour. False lashes were applied to the top lash line to accentuate this look.

A classic red pout was created with the bottom lip drawn on slightly smaller than the top lip producing an innocent Barbie-doll pout. The warm tone foundation was kept matt and heavy so the look has a B-movie colourama effect.

Photographer: Keith Clouston
Make-up: Rachel Wood using Benefit
Hair: Fabio Vivian
Model: Invlid @ M&P Models

An inspiration of Andy Warhol, Twiggy with a touch of over the top Austin Powers. A combination of benefits babe cake black wet/dry powder liner and matte white shadow was used to create a graphic pop art shaped eye. 4 layers of benefits badgal lash was applied on to the lashes and then very thick pair of fluffy false lashes were applied on top to finish the look.

Photographer: Catherine Harbour
Make-up: Rachel Wood using Benefit
Hair: Marc Eastlake using Bumble & Bumble
Model: Viktoria @ Oxygen

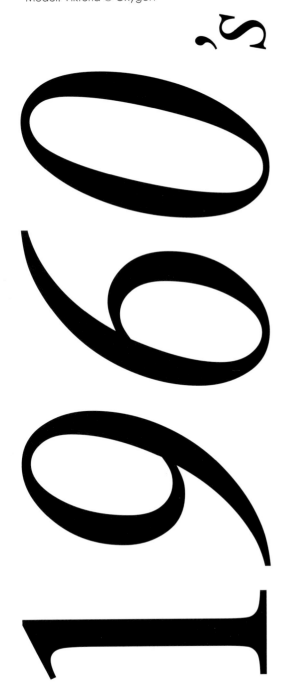

1960's

MAKEUP IS ART

70's

Photographer: Keith Clouston
Left image Make-up: Rachel Wood using Chanel
Right image Make-up Lan Nguyen using Lancome
Hair: Jana Ririnui using Babyliss Pro & Redken
Stylist: Karl Willett
Models: Pippa & Kelly @ Oxygen
Catsuit by Dior (vintage), Bangle by Freedom

80's

72

Photographer: Keith Clouston
Make-up & Hair: Lan Nguyen
using MAC & L'Oreal Professional
Stylist: Karl Willett
Model: Pippa @ Oxygen
Dress by Lucy Wrightwick, Gloves by
Gucci (vintage)

Right image:
Photographer: Catherine Harbour
Make-up Lan Nguyen using MAC
Model: Ilize Bajane @ Next

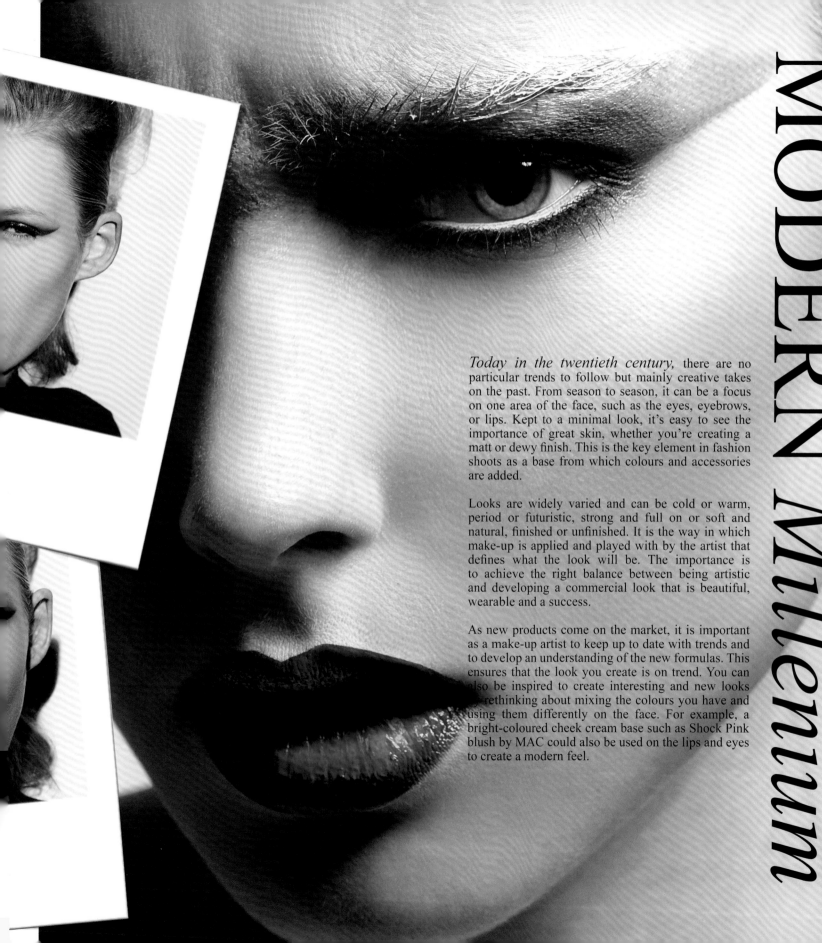

MODERN *Millenium*

Today in the twentieth century, there are no particular trends to follow but mainly creative takes on the past. From season to season, it can be a focus on one area of the face, such as the eyes, eyebrows, or lips. Kept to a minimal look, it's easy to see the importance of great skin, whether you're creating a matt or dewy finish. This is the key element in fashion shoots as a base from which colours and accessories are added.

Looks are widely varied and can be cold or warm, period or futuristic, strong and full on or soft and natural, finished or unfinished. It is the way in which make-up is applied and played with by the artist that defines what the look will be. The importance is to achieve the right balance between being artistic and developing a commercial look that is beautiful, wearable and a success.

As new products come on the market, it is important as a make-up artist to keep up to date with trends and to develop an understanding of the new formulas. This ensures that the look you create is on trend. You can also be inspired to create interesting and new looks by rethinking about mixing the colours you have and using them differently on the face. For example, a bright-coloured cheek cream base such as Shock Pink blush by MAC could also be used on the lips and eyes to create a modern feel.

RED Carpet

Red Carpet and Celebrity

When asked to do red carpet make-up, there are many factors to take into consideration. Celebrity make-up is often dictated by the celebrity's personal preference or the image that they wish to project. It is essential to research your celebrity, or client, to see if they maintain a constant image or prefer to change their look regularly. Look at the make-up they use and see where you can improve their overall look and style.

Find out what event they will be attending, and if possible, what they are wearing. Try and speak with the hairdresser and stylist to see what their ideas are and try to meet the client before the event to find out what they want.

Be armed with tear sheets and print outs of your celebrity and have a range of ideas of what you will do before arriving, show the visuals to your celebrity to ensure you are using the same terminology. You may be called to the client's house, a hotel or a salon to do your make-up. Either way, it's a good idea to do a mini-facial before starting the make-up process. It also helps to wait about 10 minutes for the creams to to be fully absorbed, so this is an ideal time for the hairdresser to start working on the hair.

You should be able to complete your make-up within 30 minutes to an hour. The make-up is nearly always glamorous and you will often be asked to recreate the classic Hollywood look, so know your periods and know what looks are popular with other celebrities. Be aware of current trends and be prepared to work at the same time as the hairdresser - celebrities are often late or working to a tight schedule.

Check your work with your own camera. The make-up should be done to last the entire event as you won't be on hand to do touch-ups later on.

Carry empty sample pots with you so you can give samples of the make-up you have used to the client, in case they want to touch-up later on. When working with a celebrity over a period of time, or when asked, be ready to advise them which products to have in their personal make-up bag. Companies will often give you free products for celebrities they want to be associated with.

You should treat this make-up as photography work. The paparazzi will be taking pictures at the event your celebrity is attending.

Photographer: Keith Clouston
Make-up: Sandra Cooke using Giorgio Armani
Hair: Natasha Mygdal using Kerastase
Model: Hollie @ IMG

EDITORIAL

Photographer: Mo Saito
Make-Up: Sandra Cooke using Becca
Hair: Zoe Irwin @ Frank
Stylist: David Hawkins @ Frank
Model: Hannah @ Next

MAKEUP IS ART

The Importance of Lighting and Make-up in Editorial Shoots

"There are so many elements that need to come together to produce a high-standard fashion editorial. Lots of planning and art direction, a good make-up artist, a stylist with the right clothing and accessories and the right models that are able to take direction and move well.

Some of the best editorial models are successful because they have a face like a blank canvas that can be molded easily into any look. Lighting needs to be well thought-out, executed and tested on the model to make sure it compliments her bone structure and shape.

Make-up is an integral part of the shoot as it brings to life the concept and creates the look and feel of the model. Photographers will use the way the light bounces off the make-up to create a polished and beautiful result. A talented make-up artist will also know how to create perfect skin and reduce the amount of retouching needed later, thus creating a better-quality image. Editorial make-up often calls for a little more creativity and is a vehicle for pushing boundaries, new looks and techniques."

Camille Sanson, photographer

"I am inspired by really strong make-up and one of the most important components of a fashion156.com shoot is to work with hugely creative make up artists. Someone who really looks at the model's face and the clothing and then decides if their ideas are actually going to work. Sometimes initial ideas need to be scrapped and an equally strong idea needs to be conceptualized and produced within minutes. So many artists I meet want to play it safe. For me, eyes, lips and cheeks can all be strong on some (many!) occasions. Preconceived ideas and rules sometimes need to be broken !"

Guy Hipwell, Editor and Creative Director fashion156.com

Photographer: Camille Sanson
Make-up: Lan Nguyen using Mac
Hair: Andrea Cossolari
Stylist: Svetlana Prodanic
Model: Kate Willing

Blue dress Inbarspectar, Jacket
Manish Arora.

MAKEUP IS ART

What does a stylist need or look for in a make up artist?

"Let's just assume the make up artist can do the basics - beautiful skin. And they are really creative. Then, the other qualities I think a make-up artist has to have is to be well organised, have a team they can trust and they need to know about trends. Not just make up trends but also fashion and colour trends. A make-up artist, like the stylist, needs to be able to look at a selection of clothes and offer a variety of make-up looks. Often a junior make-up artist will ask "What do you want?" I like a make-up artist who can offer suggestions and isn't just an order taker. I'll make a mood board to give the team a vision and direction but often the make-up artist will make one too. A beauty story can start with the vision of the make-up artist and they'll present a mood board. From there I can suggest the jewellery, accessories etc.

I like to work with the same team because I can trust them. My work can be quite varied, from commercial to catwalk, so I need a make-up artist who is strong on many levels. She also needs to be personable. Once you know someone who can do the job it becomes all about personality - do you get along with them, are they the right fit? There are so many good make up artists, so it can come down to having a similar vision - do they contribute to the team, are they responsible and fun to work with?"

By Rebekah Roy Fashion stylist

MAKEUP IS ART

Photographer: Camille Sanson
Make-up: Lan Nguyen using MAC
Hair: Andrea Cassolari
Stylist: Nasrin Jean-Baptiste
Model: Elena @ Oxygen

82

Dress by Bernard Chandran
Bracelet by J.W. Anderson
Shoes by Modernist
All headwear customised by stylist
from a selection at Angels

MAKEUP IS ART

Lace body con jumpsuit stylist own.
Skirt by Topshop. Gloves by Gloved Up

Jacket by Louise Amstrup
Dress by Ashish Bracelets by Disaya

MAKEUP IS ART

Photographer: Camille Sanson
Make-up: Philippe Miletto @ Terri Tanaka
Hair: Andrea Cassolari
Stylist: Nasrin Jean-Baptiste
Model: Erin @ Nevs
Shirt by Bora Aksu

MAKEUP IS ART

N⁰5

"The story was about a young woman who arrives in London and checks herself in to the boutique No.5 Cavendish Square hotel for the night, Having been stood up by her date, she decides to have a wild night of her own. We wanted to achieve a sense of opulence and indulgence and where possible use Swarovski crystals. We spent four days crystallising fruit, champagne bottles, bowls, eggs and chocolate, hand applying each 3mm crystal. A tight budget meant we had to draw on every creative resource to get as much sumptuous fabric and as many crystals to dress the bedroom, bathroom and club. Breakfast in Bed was when the beautiful girl wakes up... has a bath... and goes back to a bed of lush black velvet and liquid gold fabric... to find a huge ornate silver tray bursting with treats of Swarovski crystal eggs, apples, pomegranates and pears... cherries piled high on crystal ice cubes... crystal bowls of strawberries dusted with crystal sugar dust... a crystallised cakes stand piled high with Lauderee Macaroons in pinks and blues and gold...fine china tea cups... gold plated spoons in a bowl of crystal sugar cubes.... a wondrous sparkling feast for the eyes.....a glittering start to the day...."

Set Designer, Misty Buckley

A night at No5 Cavendish Square London

The process of working from a fresh idea through to seeing the final story for an editorial piece is always exciting. Even though you have a vision in your head, sometimes the outcome may not be what you expected due to many factors. You may run out of time because of unexpected challenges, which can slow the day down, so it is important the team is there for support and you must be prepared to be able to offer alternative ideas on the day. With careful planning, you tend to end up with something much better than you visualised to begin with.

Before the shoot, prep work will have started weeks before, from devising a theme, to choosing the clothes, brands, make-up looks, lighting and sourcing the right location. These are all the key factors with an editorial shoot. You have an art director, make-up artist, hair stylist, fashion stylist, model and photographer.

Art in motion: creative brief for clients
For a project working for Swarovski crystals, we came up with the idea of two modern, luxurious women looking beautiful on a night out and enjoying the lavish lifestyle surrounded by crystals.

The sets were designed and sketched out with possible scenes. In order to successfully convey the luxury branding behind the advert, the perfect location chosen to support this was the exclusive hotel No 5 Cavendish Square in London. All the rooms were perfect for the setting we had envisaged - dark and decadent – and the props all tied in perfectly with each room. All the props had been covered in crystals - by hand - and took most of the day to set up.

The model had been selected at an earlier stage through a casting and speaking process with the model agency. It is important the model has the right character and look for the shoot.

Make-up for this shoot was used to create a look that was timelessly elegant and groomed. The model's features were quite soft and delicate and so in order to make her look stronger, the eyebrows were groomed with an eyebrow gel and once dried, lightened with full-coverage foundation. The eyes were contoured and defined with a mixture of cream and matt eye shadows. Lips are natural matt to begin with and then darkened with a stronger colour to emphasise the change of scene and model.

The model's hair was left down to work with all the hats and kept well groomed with a 1940's air of elegance.

The lighting was moody, but had a lot of reflection from the garments and the crystals were brightened and enhanced by post-production retouching.

89

Photographer: Camille Sanson
Make-up: Lan Nguyen using Mac & Swarovski
Hair: Marc Eastlake using Bumble & Bumble
Stylist: Shyla Hassan
Set Designer: Misty Buckley
Set Assistants: Richard Olivieri & Reggie Matheson
Model: Birgit @ First Model Management
Photography Assistants Pau Cegarra & Laurie Noble
Make-up Assistant: Karla Barchieri @ AOFM Agency
Special thanks to Mark Whittle at No. 5.

Dress Ruth Tavardos worn with Corset Ericson
Beamon, Shoes Gil Carvalho,

MAKEUP IS ART

Hat by swarovski, Jumper Jullian Macdonald for Swarovski, Shoes Gil Carvalho, Jewellery Ericson Beamon

Red Dress Ruth Tarvydas, Head band Louis Marriette, Jewellery Ericson Beamon

94

BEAUTY *Editorial*

For the fashion world, the editorial is the equivalent of a good book, it tells a story, but instead of words, creatives use clothes, hair, make-up, photography and lighting to convey a message. Editorials can range from just a few pages shot in a studio with different outfits, to large twelve-plus spreads shot at an exotic location.

The most important part of working on an editorial is working as a team. All the elements need to work together harmoniously to achieve that perfect shot.

Photographer: Camille Sanson
Make-up: Lan Nguyen using Dior
Hair: Kuni Kohzaki
Model: Daniel Foster

Post Production

A photographer's job extends beyond standing behind the lens and capturing the shots. When everyone's working day is over, the photographer must start work on the post-production process.

Post production is the general term used to describe the process of turning the raw shots from the camera on the day of the photo shoot, to the polished, glossy images that we see in magazines.

The first step of post production is the selection of images. Often hundreds of images are taken in any one day of shooting, so narrowing down to the best image(s) is a large job, with often only miniscule differences between the shots. The team, including hair, make-up and styling may help with this process, narrowing down to a smaller number of potential final images. Once the final images are selected, retouching is carried out to perfect and tweak the image.

98

Post production, selecting images
Retouching has become a widely standardised practice in magazines and advertising campaigns, in order to smooth out wrinkles, fine lines, lumps, bumps and blemishes in the skin. It can also be used to stretch out models, slim models down and remove cellulite, which can result in an unrealistic picture of beauty.

What it means to the make-up artist
This allows small errors to be rectified, for example, when a model's lipstick has faded in a corner, or a few stray hairs need to be removed, or there are clumps of mascara. Retouching can lead to sloppiness as some make-up artists may feel they don't have to work hard to perfect their make-up application.

Although the responsibility of retouching belongs to the photographer, the make-up artist should review and make sure they are happy with the images that are projecting their work and ensure that the make-up hasn't been completely altered.

Photographer: Camille Sanson
Make-up: Lan Nguyen using Dior
Hair: Kuni Kohzaki
Model: Daniel Foster

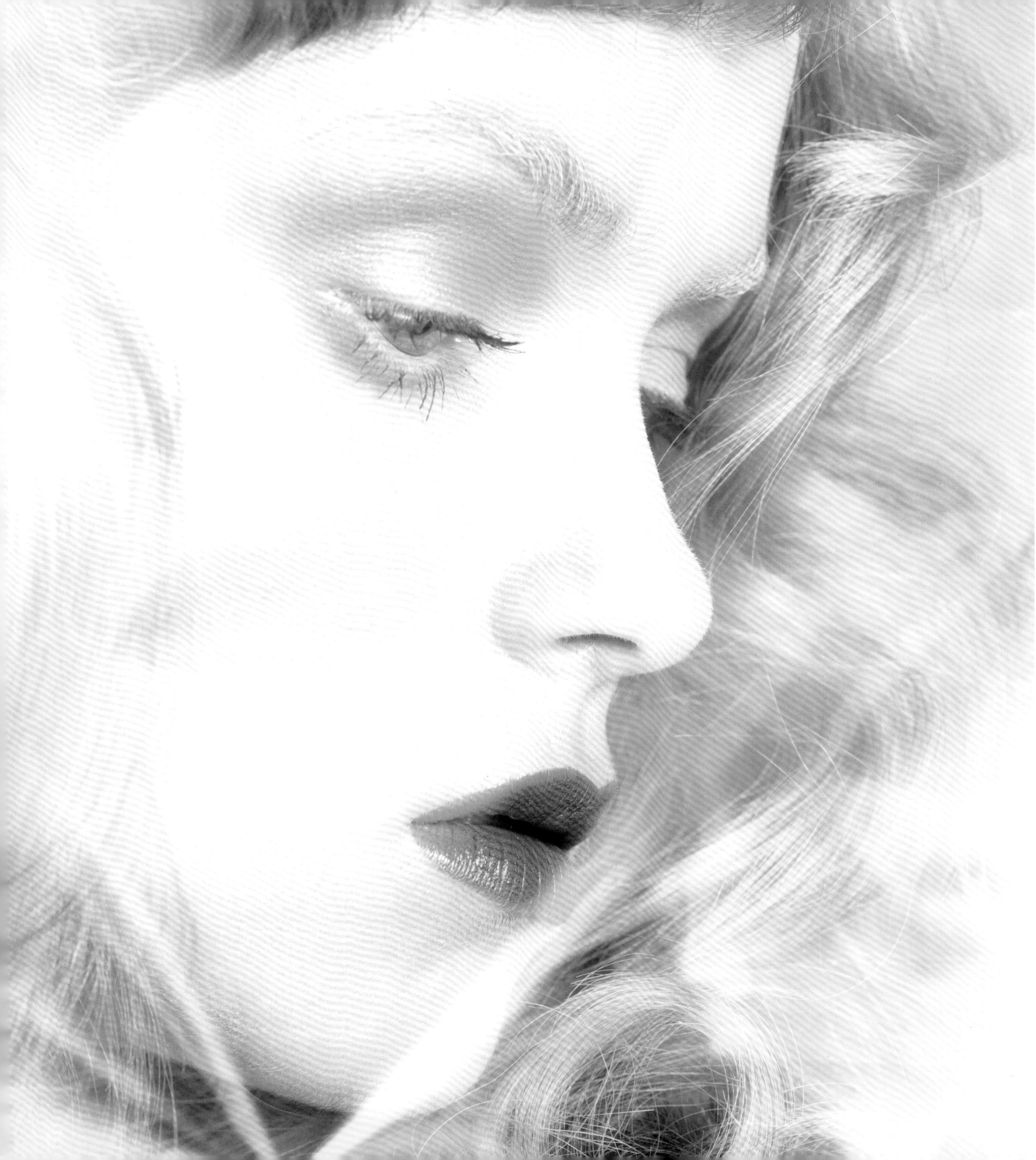

ADVERTISING

Make-up artists are almost always used in advertising. An example of this may be the appearance of sweat on the brow of a sportsman in a Nike commercial or the pigtails on a little girl in a toy advert.

From the commercial adverts you see on TV to the billboard posters on the tube; a make-up artist was there on the shoot insuring the people being photographed or filmed are looking their best. The look or type of make-up a make-up artist will do on the "talent" (what the model, actor, person etc is referred to on set) is job specific.

The make-up look not only has to fit in with the story of the advertisement but also has to be appropriate for the product that the advertisement is trying to push.

Photographer: Camille Sanson
Make-up: Lan Nguyen using Lancome
Hair: Marc Eastlake
Stylist: Shyla Hassan
Model: Sabrina @ Next
Dress by Bora Aksu

102

Photographer: Camille Sanson
Make-up: Lan Nguyen using Shu Uemura
Hair: Andrea Cassolari
Model: Hannah @ Next

104

Conceptual

Avant-garde make-up is as infinite as one's imagination. It's all about pushing the boundaries and encourages you to think outside the box.

Prime examples of this type of make-up look can often be seen on the catwalk at Paris couture fashion week.

Designers such as John Galliano and Jean Paul Gaultier are some of the leading trendsetters of this look.

Many designers showcase their work to demonstrate their individuality and cutting-edge values. Often, their clothes are considered to be more like wearable art. Therefore, the make-up designs that complement the clothes can also be seen as quirky and beautiful art works.

The concept of the make-up designs, the colours used and how and where the make-up is applied can influence the commercial market, too, and inspire the creation of new make-up products. Brands including Charles Fox, MAC and Shu Uemura are constantly developing interesting make-up ideas for the professional artists. This constant stream of development means there is no limit to what you can create.

The catwalk shows also inspire the future trends and avant-garde editorials in magazines. High fashion magazines such as Numero, 10, Dazed & Confused and Pop are just some of the many magazines that take inspiration from the catwalk and then create their own images for the public domain, and ultimately feed the make-up and styling world with even more new creative imagery and iconic looks.

106

Photographer: Fabrice Lachant
Make-up: Lan Nguyen using MAC
Hair: Marc Eastlake
Model: Monika R @ Next
Left to right: Fashion Pieces using
Metro newspaper, mask using
Swarovski all by Marc Eastlake

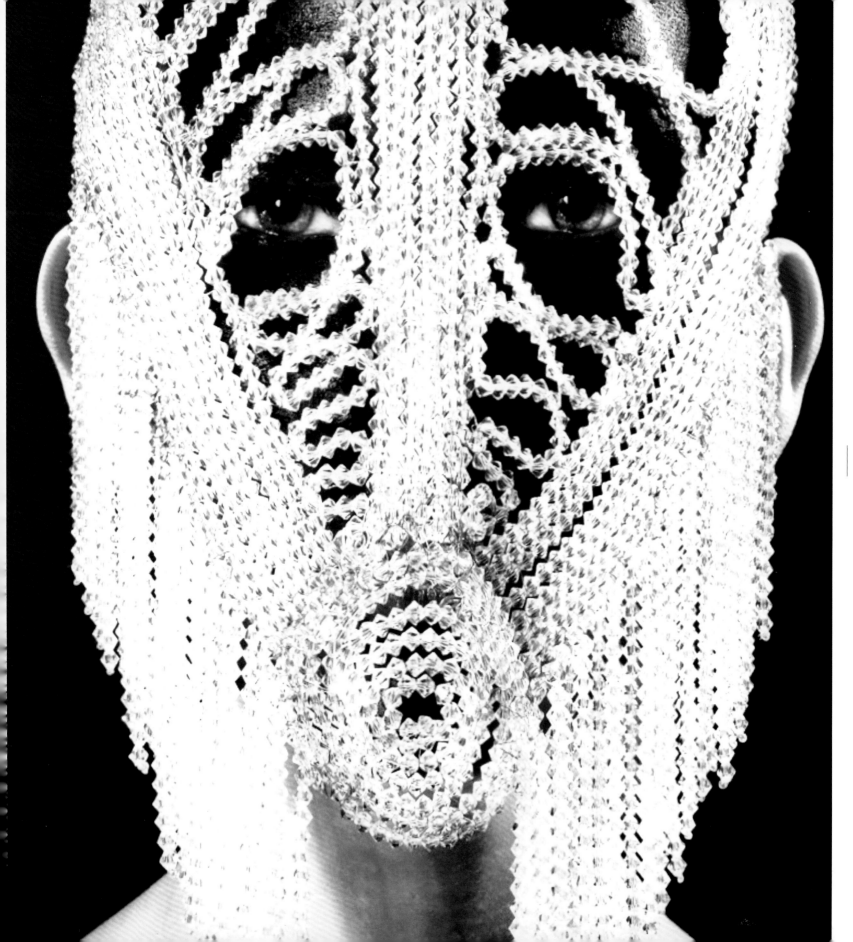

108

110

Photographer: Catherine Harbour
Make-up: Philippe Miletto using MAC
Hair: Andrea Cassolari
Model Iliza @ Next

MAKEUP IS ART

Photographer: Catherine Harbour
Make-up: Lan Nguyen using MAC
Hair: Marc Eastlake using Bumble & Bumble
Set Design: Dominic Elvin
Model: Mika

114

Photographer: Camille Sanson
Make-up: Lan Nguyen using MAC
Hair: Marc Eastlake using Bumble & Bumble
Styling: Shyla Hassan
Model: Sara Amos @ INC

From left to right: Blue dress by Bernard Chandran, Jewelery by Erickson Beamon. Mesh top with gold spots by Topshop, Peach blouse stylists own, Skirt by William Tempest. Black dress by William Tempest, jewelery by Erickson Beamon. Navy waistcoat by Modernist, cream shorts by Bernard Chandran, jewelery by Erickson Beamon. Head pieces by Marc Eastlake

Salvador Dali
Photography & Styling: Camille Sanson
Make-up & Styling: Lan Nguyen using MAC
Hair: Andrea Cassolari
Models: Hannah @ Next & Claudia @ Nevs

Photographer: Fabrice Lachant
Make-up: Lan Nguyen using MAC
Hair: Marc Eastlake using Bumble & Bumble
Model: Renee Mansbridge

BODY Art

Body art is one of the oldest forms of art

Historically it has been a tradition of many ancient tribes across the globe using materials such as coloured clay and charcoal mixtures. It has now entered the mainstream and is used in mediums such as advertising campaigns, on album covers and fashion shows.

Body painting is becoming an increasingly competitive industry and it is important to have the skills needed before taking on any professional jobs, as good-quality body painting is not something you can easily achieve without plenty of practice.

Techniques and equipment

There are two main techniques associated with body painting; brush and sponge painting and airbrushing. It is far easier to start body painting with a few simple brushes and sponges and work with face paints. A basic kit will consist of a selection of primary and basic colours such as black, white, red, yellow and blue. You don't want to spend all of your time mixing, so green, purple, pink, orange, grey and brown are also handy staples in your kit.

Brushes

When choosing your brushes, look out for ones with dense bristles, as it will lessen streaking, and make sure you have a selection of different sizes to choose from.
It is also helpful to have a brush with a curved edge as these create smoother, lines.

Tips: A flat, straight-edged brush will help you create well-defined lines.

- A large flat brush that is at least 2 inches wide or more helps cover large areas of the body quickly.

- A medium-sized flat-edged brush and a small, flat-edged brush (square to rectangular in shape) creates straight lines and crisp edges.

It is also handy to have a brush with a fine point as this will allow you to do more detailed work, as well as working from a thick line to a thin one.

Face painting sponges can be used to blend colours on the body, cover underwear in paint and get paint into awkward areas, especially around the eye area.

Using the paints

Body paint is water based and it's important to know how the paints work in order to get the most out of them. Because the paints are activated with water, you will find that when you try to layer your colours, they may start to blend into one another. For example, if you paint white detail over a black background, you will quickly discover that the bright white turns grey.

It is much easier to cover a lighter colour with a darker colour than the other way around. When it is necessary to paint a lighter colour over a darker one, then fix your base coat with a fixing spray or strong hold hairspray. This will help to eliminate blending problems.

Tip: It's important to get a really creamy consistency to your paint in order to get an even finish. The easiest way to blend your colours is to do it when they are still wet. The best way to avoid tell-tale join marks is by covering your largest areas such as the chest and back first, and then finish by joining the painting at the sides where it will be a lot less noticeable to clients and photographers.

Airbrushing

It is expensive buying all the necessary equipment that you will need, but there are also other tools that can be used to create dramatic effects when a paintbrush won't do. An airbrushing kit consists of a compressor, an airbrush gun and paints.
Airbrushing is an extremely useful skill to have when you work on jobs that require a lot of stencilling to be done and when you want very softly blended highlights and shadows.

To use an airbrush gun you push down on the trigger to start the airflow and pull back to release the paint. The lighter you press the trigger, the softer the airflow, and the more you pull back on the trigger, the more paint is released.

Once you get used to the way your gun works you'll be able to create anything from a line as thick as a hair's width to a smooth and perfectly blended background. Practice on cheap canvases and with acrylic paint to build up your skills, and when you can get a willing model try to practice on a body so that you get used to working on a living, breathing - and sometimes moving -canvas!

Ensuring the job goes smoothly
When you're planning your body paint, think about the order in which you want to cover the body. When body paint is dry it is relatively touch-proof, but it will smudge easily if rubbed. It is often best, if working with a female model, to cover their breasts first so she feels less exposed and more comfortable. This is also useful in creating a good working relationship with your model.

It's important to leave certain areas of the body such as the mouth, hands and bottom, clean or without detail initially, as most detailed body paints will take between 3 to 6 hours to be completed and during this time, your model will probably need to sit down, eat, drink and use the bathroom.

Some models will struggle having to stand up for such long periods of time without moving, so make sure you have sugary snacks and drinks on hand to keep your model's energy levels up. Some models might not want to drink a lot of water because they are worried about needing to visit the toilet and smudging the paint, so be sure to reassure them that it is a lot easier to clean up smudged paint than having to clean off an entire section because your model has fainted!

When you are working as an artist you must know the paint's limitations as well as your own. Work a design through with a client from their initial concept to the final approved design. This way, you will be sure that what you are producing is according to plan, you will feel confident in doing a great job and ultimately, you will produce an amazing piece of art.

To get repeat business, you must remember that you are only ever as good as your last job.

Photographer: George Kuchler
Right to left Make-up: Carolyn Roper using MAC (two times body painter world champion) & Craig Tracy
Models: Carolyn Roper & Craig Tracy

Photographer: Catherine Harbour
Make-up: Lan Nguyen using MAC
Stencilling: Carolyn Roper
Hair: Andrea Callosari
Model: Kate Willing
Headpiece by Dominic Elvin

Stencils were used to create an image of a girl trapped inside a snow globe, but instead of snow falling all around her the snowflakes are on her.

White-coloured hairspray was painted through snowflake stencils to create an airbrushed effect.
White glitter was then applied on top using a touch of Duo eyelash glue to keep it in place.

A mixture of pink, pearl and lavender eye shadows were then blended on the face to create a cold look to the model's skin.
MAC Strobe Cream was also blended into a pale tone of MAC Face and Body Foundation

Photographer: Keith Clouston
Make-up: Rachel Wood using MAC
Hair: Fabio Vivian
Model: Invlid at M& P models

Collaborating

"Collaborating with make-up artists is always different, depending on what the brief is. For instance, when I am shooting for the British Hairdressing Awards, it's predominately about the hair, so the relationship is with a team of people and the mood board. The mood board will dictate the feeling of the whole shoot, ensuring the make-up artist, photographer, fashion stylist as well as the hairdresser are all singing from the same hymn sheet. Sometimes the hairdresser will know what they want from the make-up, other times they won't, so the make-up artist will have more input to the design of the make-up.

Sometimes on a hair shoot, it may not be clear what is wanted with the make-up, so there will either be a prep day in advance or the team will arrive early and play with the make-up to see what works. This way there is plenty of scope for individual creativity and freedom.

Fashion shoots are totally different, especially if it's a test shoot. Everyone experiments and is pushing the boundaries in their own field, but the team comes together for the overall look – it's not just about one person, it's a collective effort.

When doing fashion shows, the focus is on the clothes. Before the show there will be a fitting where the head hair stylist and make-up artist create their looks on a model and present them to the designer to see if it works. If the designer is happy, then the heads go back to their teams and brief them with the look. This needs to be done very quickly, so there is very little time for prepping and often the hair and make-up is being done at the same time. The make-up artist needs to work in tandem with the hairdresser and vice versa.

When working with celebrities, they dictate their image so you have to liaise with make-up and styling. It's all about what the celebrity wants and creating an overall image, so you may be recreating a style they are known for rather than having creative input."

Desmond Murray, celebrity photographer and hair stylist

Photography & Hair: Desmond Murray
Make-up: Jo Sugar using Charles Fox
Model: Sophie Willing

UNDERWATER

There are many different scenarios when waterproof make-up is going to be required. You could be shooting on a beach, in a swimming pool or filming in a water tank on a film set. In most cases, the model will need to be retouched after just one shot in the water.

Working with water can be unpredictable and it's not always easy to guess how the skin is going to look or react when make-up and water meet, so be prepared to make changes.

The key to using and working with waterproof make-up successfully is how you apply and set it afterwards. It is important that all the skin on show is covered with foundation or a

waterproof fake tan. Finish the skin with a specialist fixer spray and powder, which will help the make-up stay on longer in water. Sometimes a few blasts of hairspray can also do the trick.

Water reflects light and, depending on the type of shoot you are working on, the water can alter the colour of the skin, making it looked washed-out and colourless. This is especially true when working in deep water tanks. For best results and to combat this, use cream-based products and strong vibrant colours to bring out the features. By mixing mediums in with eye pigments it will give you a longer-lasting look, but these will tend to crack when worn all day.

Photographer: Fabrice Lachant
Make-up: Lan Nguyen using MAC
Model: Kate Willing
Make-up Assistants: Kelly Mendiola
& Karla B @ AOFM Agency

Adornment

Make-up is evolving all the time and continues to be very experimental. By adorning the skin and using techniques of mixing paint and pigments you can create mask-like effects, which are visually inspiring. This can usually be seen in creative magazines and in jewellery adverts where the face and piece of jewellery is the focus of the image.

There are alternative materials that can look interesting when applied to areas of the face such as fabrics, beads, crystals, feathers and most art and craft materials.

Crystals add a touch of glamour to a look and when applied sparsely around the eye area can be wearable for a special occasion. For the best results, only use a small amount of glue, too much will cause the stone to move and become messy. Duo glue can be used to stick materials such as these to the skin as it is safe and easy to remove afterwards.

Photographer: Camille Sanson
Make-up: Lan Nguyen using MAC & Swarovski
Hair: Marc Eastlake
Model: Birgit @ First Model Management
Photography Assistant Pau Cegarra
Make-up Assistant: Karla Barchieri @ AOFM Agency
Headpiece by Marc Eastlake using Swarovski

Mixers
Mixing mediums can change the texture and create new colours of a product. There are different kinds of mixing mediums available such as lash, eyeliner, face and body, and lips. By mixing in the lash mixing medium, available at MAC stores, you can create your own mascaras.

For best results mix the pigment evenly until it is a paste before applying.

Photographer: Camille Sanson
Make-up: Lan Nguyen using MAC & Swarovski
Jewelery by Louis Mariette
Model: Ida @ Oxygen

Photographer: Camille Sanson
Make-up: Lan Nguyen using MAC
Hair: Andrea Cassolari
Stylist: Nasrin Jean-Baptiste
Models Left to right:
Elena @ Oxygen & Kate Willing

136

Tools

Tools
A make-up artist's kit is not just comprised of make-up, but also a large selection of tools. These are essential to make the job easier and allow the correct application of make-up.

Eyelash curlers
Eyelash curlers are also an essential item in a make-up artist's kit, with the most popular brand being Shu Uemura. Eyelash curlers need to be used before mascara, and for maximum impact, used as close to the eyelid as possible (without pinching the skin). Heated eyelash curlers are available on the market and can be used to curl stubborn, straight lashes. It is possible to heat metal eyelash curlers using a hairdryer, but these need to be tested for temperature on the inner forearm prior to applying to the eye. Mini eyelash curlers, such as ones by Shu Uemura, are great for curling the odd, stubborn straight lash.

Tweezers
Besides tidying up eyebrows, tweezers are needed applying false lashes and working with latex glue, such as Duo. Make-up artists will also use their tweezers and Duo for applying intricate crystal, bead and feather work on the face.

Masking tape
Masking tape is handy to have in any make-up artist's kit to remove any glitter fallout stuck to the face or clothes. It can also be used to create precise straight lines or graphic shapes on the face.

Bags
The most efficient way to transport all the make-up a professional make-up artist needs for a job is in a suitcase on wheels. Not only does it hold all the kit you need (and spares), but it helps protect your body as you are not carrying the full weight of it all. Most make-up artists will organise their kit into clear make-up bags, with similar products grouped together, to be able to see all products available and know where to find products easily and quickly.
Other essentials

For a full kit, you will also need the disposables, such a tissues, cotton buds, cotton pads, baby wipes (handy for cleaning hands and kit), and basic face wipes (such as Simple) when make-up needs to be removed quickly.

Photographer: Camille Sanson
Make-up: Lan Nguyen using Shu Uemura
Model: Erin @ Nevs

AOFM PRO

Brushes

Brushes are probably the most important tools in a make-up artist's kit. Not only do brushes help apply make-up with accuracy and precision, but allow the artist to blend and move the product to create the desired effect.

Make-up brushes come in a variety of different hair types, as well as sizes and shapes for different types of make-up application. The product formula determines which brush hair is suitable for use. Most make-up artists will have a large selection of brushes, and sometimes several of the same of their favourite brushes.

Brush cleaner

Brush cleaner is essential for cleaning brushes in between make-up application for use on different models. This is both to remove product and sanitise the brushes. A good, simple alcohol-based brush cleaner, such as Isopropyl alcohol will kill all bacteria instantly, and dry within a few seconds, ready for re-use.

Clockwise from top left – Pro Crease brush, AOFM Pro Concealor brush (Large), Pro Wide blending brush, Pro slanted blending brush, Pro Eyeshadow application brush 2, Pro Eyeshadow application brush 3, Pro Eyeshadow application brush 4, Prof Eyeshadow brush 5, Pro flat end blending brush, Pro Foundation brush, Pro Liquid Foundation brush, Pro Bronze & Shading brush, Pro Contour brush, Pro Eyebrow and Eyelash comb, Pro fan contour & shading brush, Pro smudge brush, Pro eyeliner brush, Pro loose powder brush, Pro 3 in 1 brush, Pro eyeshadow application brush 1, Pro lip brush, Pro slanted fine brow brush, Pro Signature fan brush, Pro concealor brush (small).

Set including brush belt bag available from www.aofmpro.com

CATWALK
& *Backstage*

Behind the scenes

What really happens before you see a runway show from either sitting on the front row, on the television or on the pages of a glossy magazine, can sometimes be taken for granted if you are not involved in the process. It takes dedication and months of hard work to prepare for such an event.

A long time before a model even sets foot on the catwalk there are meetings to discuss the trend forecasts, concepts and designs. Models, locations and crews have to be picked and tested and then the PR teams have to go into overdrive to make sure that key press teams come and cover the event. It is a cycle that has been going on for many seasons and one that will never change, and as a make-up artist you can't help but want to be a part of it all.

A make-up artist has an important role in the catwalk show, as it is their responsibility to make sure that the look complements the designer's collection without overpowering it and taking the attention away from the garments. The look needs to be beautiful and fresh, but it needs to be as new and exciting as the clothes as these looks will be the guidelines for next season's trends. Beauty editors, from across the world, will be using snapshots of the catwalk shows as references in their editorial - and not to forget the celebrities that are in the front row. If they see a look they like then you never know what may happen.

The head make-up artist for the show will have spent weeks designing mood boards, collaborating with the chief designer, fashion stylist and hair stylist to come up with the various looks. The head make-up artist will then demonstrate the look to the rest of the team. Many of the assistants will take a Polaroid of the look to then use as a reference guide in order to recreate the look. All the artists then work on their model. It is important that the looks are finished on time and are on spec, as there is nothing worse than seeing the mistakes on stage. There is then a make-up test and full dress rehearsal.

It is important to be focused when working on a catwalk show as backstage can be very chaotic with television crews interviewing stylists and the designers, beauty editors wanting to get a preview, photographers getting close-ups of the make-up and models running in and out, getting their hair done and having clothes fittings. There are always elements that you cannot plan for, but have to deal with the best way possible, such as a model arriving late or having bad skin. However, when the music starts, the lights dim and the first model walks down the runway and everyone looks at something that you have helped create, you realise it's all been worth it.

143

Backstage Etiquette

One of the best things a new make-up artist can do to advance their career is to assist an established make-up artist. They can learn new creative ideas, innovative ways to use their brushes and see what products other make-up artists favour in their kits. Most importantly they learn the proper etiquette for being backstage at a fashion show or what is really required from the make-up artist on a photo shoot.

Helpful Hints to being a good make-up assistant

Show up with clean brushes and a basic make-up kit. Most of the time, especially on fashion shows, the head make-up artist will provide or have the key products required to complete the look.

Don't be late and try to be early if possible; a make up artist usually will be the first person on a job. It's important to be set up and ready to go for when the model arrives. If the shoot is a magazine cover with a celebrity, you wouldn't want the star waiting for you! If a make-up assistant is working on a fashion show, they must be there on time to learn the brief or the "look" for the job.

Listen to instructions from the head make-up artist, the most frustrating thing for the head make-up artist is for their assistant to go off and do their own thing. If a client has asked for a particular look on a job and the make-up artist does a beautiful make-up but it doesn't fulfil the brief they can lose the job or never be hired again.

If you are standing around doing nothing always ask the make-up artist what else can be done. Cleaning brushes, making a cup of tea, holding hair pins are all tedious jobs but need to be done and are always very much appreciated on set. Doing those extra little things will make you stand out from other less-helpful assistants.

If you are assisting, you are working on the head make up artist's job and with their clients. Behaving with a mature and professional attitude is essential. You should not be giving the client your make-up card for future work-; that is seen as trying to steal a client from the head make up artist and is definitely frowned upon. A make-up assistant's behaviour is a reflection on the make up artist.

If you are booked to assist on a job and something comes up so you are unable to do it always call the make-up artist as soon as possible, do not text or send an email. Picking up the phone is the professional thing to do, better yet suggest a replacement if possible. Keeping a good network of other make up artists is a great way to boost your own career as often make-up artists get double booked and having a good circle of contacts generates more work for everyone.

Most established make up artists receive about 3 emails a week from new make-up artists or students enquiring about assisting. So never forget that make up assistants are easily replaced, but a great assistant is invaluable.

How do I become a successful make-up artist?

Training, assisting, testing and practicing are all key to becoming successful, however being dedicated, having great contacts and continually networking are also essential elements to ensure you have a good chance of doing well as a make-up artist.

Training- Do I need a qualification to work in the make-up industry?

There is no standard form of accepted qualification in the freelance make-up industry. Many schools have their own form of certificate or offer NVQ, BABTAC and BTEC certificates. However, there are no requirements in the industry to work as a professional make-up artist, and in fact, this does not guarantee work, as there is no standard governing body. It really depends on the type of work you are pursuing.

If you are looking to join a make-up agency, work on a photo shoot with a new photographer or on a catwalk show, then you will be asked for your portfolio as proof of work and skills. Sometimes you will be asked to demonstrate your ideas or test the look before the actual shoot day. Your portfolio is really the only form of qualification accepted, especially within the fashion industry.

If you're seeking work with a make-up brand on a counter, companies prefer their sales staff to have some make-up training, but again it is not essential, as they would get the brand's make-up artist tutor to go through the techniques and concept of the looks that they want you to sell to the customer. Often there will be a few training days to show you the new products and trends for the season.

If you are working in the beauty, film and TV industry in licensed premises, you may be asked to show both your qualifications and a CV. In film and TV, a show reel will often be requested.

What does working freelance mean?

Working freelance is the same as being self-employed. It requires you to set up your own business and register your chosen name as a registered company. You pay your own salary and work directly with the client. Then you are in charge of paying your income tax and national insurance. Being freelance, you have the freedom to do whatever job you like and work when you want to work. However, you have to be aware that you don't get the perks of being signed to a contract, where you would get holiday pay or sick pay.

If you don't work, you don't get paid, it's as simple as that. You always need to plan ahead for your next job so your diary is filled and you keep working. It is easy to get de-motivated and tiresome when you have to do all the paperwork and try and find work and also to be creative at the same time.

Being signed to a contract with a make-up agency offers you the security of having someone looking to help you grow and build your profile. They deal with all the admin side of your work, such as invoices and payments. They will also organise your diary and keep you in the heart of the industry, which isn't easy since there are so many artists trying to do the same thing.

How does a new make-up artist get an agent?

Getting an agent can be very competitive. There are very few spaces per agency, but usually once a make-up artist lands one, it is much easier to get into another. A good way for a new make-up artist to get into an agency is to call them up and let them know they have just finished a make-up course and are available for assisting work. It is a good idea for the make-up artist to have worked on a few tests first before approaching an agent, as they will probably ask to see their work. Very often, once a make-up artist is on an assistant list and they do well, there is room to move up into the agency in a shorter space of time.

How do I know where to get the best training possible?

If you are looking for a make-up school, there are several points to consider before doing so. The make-up industry is hard and very competitive; this cannot be stressed or highlighted enough times. There are many schools claiming to promise the world, however, it's up to you to create a successful career for yourself as a working make-up artist. No school can promise every student success.

Many make-up schools claim to offer working make-up artists as tutors. Always ask to see the school tutor's current portfolios. If they can't supply one, then it is doubtful as to if they are current working fashion make-up artists. If they do supply one, then look closely - if they are not credited in a magazine or of magazine-quality, then they are not really top working make-up artists.
It's no guarantee that schools with great pictures on their site use good, make-up tutors who are active in the industry. Ask who will be teaching you and then do your research on the tutor via the internet.

See who supports the school - this can include big name cosmetic brands and hair companies. Any good school will be affiliated and working with big name companies as this shows they are highly regarded within the industry.

If you are looking at schools claiming to offer international certificates that will ensure you will get work abroad afterwards, be wary as there is no such thing as a fully qualified make-up artist, whether this is on a national or international basis. A certificate alone will not guarantee work. There is no recognised international make-up association or qualification. The only association recognised by the leading UK schools is NASMAH (the National Association of Screen Make Up and Hair, www.nasmah.co.uk.)

Schools are set up to act as a means of access to fast-track knowledge and understanding of the industry - they don't qualify you to work. There are a number of top make-up artists in the industry working in magazines like Vogue and TV and feature films with no previous make-up training, but who have gone on to be very successful.

Find out what cosmetic brands the school offers you to work with during your training. If a school only offers one brand, you will be stuck in the industry, as no make-up artist will ever use just one brand. Your training should give you an understanding of all the products a professional would use. Be cautious of schools that offer kits, as in many cases they are not professional products and you can end up in a situation where you are not confident or comfortable using these products. Once you complete your training, you should have a good working knowledge of beauty products.

It is important to see what past students have achieved from the school or ask to meet current students, as this will give you a good insight if the school offers the right education for you. Student testimonials mean nothing and can be manipulated to sound better, so it is a must to get all the facts right before you decide to part with your money.

Often on a course, you will be offered the chance to shoot your own portfolio to get you started and this will mean working with a model and photographer. It is important that you see the quality of images from past students, because this shoot will be the first image you have to showcase your work. Can you visualise it in a magazine? Does the model look professional?

As a student, you are paying a lot of money for your training - you deserve to get the best teachers, products to work with and after care that money can buy.

Many students assume that a career within the make-up industry comes straightaway after training. This is often not the case, as you still need to build up your practical experience.

Now I have trained, what is the best way to build a professional make-up kit?

Putting together a professional make-up kit when starting out can seem daunting and costly, but build it up slowly and it won't be as scary as you may think. When starting out, it's important not to buy the most expensive materials until you need them. It is advisable that students buy good-quality foundations, concealers and eye shadows with good strong pigment as a base first. As for lip glosses and lipsticks and other bits and pieces, it is better to go for a cheaper version to start with and invest in them as you get more experienced. When you start working with big name designers and magazines and high-profile events, many press agents for cosmetic companies will give you products in return for credits, which is also a form of advertising for the brand.

How does a new make-up artist build up their portfolio?

After gaining make-up training, new make-up artists then work on tests. These are unpaid photos shoots organised between the photographer, stylist, make-up artist and sometimes a hairdresser. The aim of a test is to produce new photographs that showcase the work of all of those involved. On a test, model agencies often supply one of their new faces for the shoot to help build up their book as well. From there, it is up to the individual make-up artist to contact the modeling agencies, letting them know that they have just finished a make-up course and that they are available to show their work from the shoot. In turn, the agencies will often call new make-up artists to work on tests with their models.

There are also lots of great internet sites with postings from photographers looking for make-up artists to collaborate with on tests. Here, new make-up artists can also post their work credits and portfolio pictures. Remember, your portfolio is your tool in guaranteeing you future work, but it's just as important to have business cards to hand while networking, as you never know who you might meet. A large volume of the work freelancers get are usually by chance meetings, word of mouth and through friends.

It is also good practice to have a website to showcase your work. The more people know that you exist, the more work you will get and a better profile.

How can I get to assist a make-up artist?

Usually when you have finished your training, you will have been given experience to assist your tutors on jobs. Some schools have an after care service where they will direct you to the right places for contacts and make-up agencies. It is up to you to motivate yourself and offer your time and help to a current working make-up artist.

It is important to try and get work with as many different artists as possible to gain tips from them. Every make-up artist has their own style and steps to create a look, even if the outcome is the same. There are so many different techniques and clever shortcuts that only you can learn from as an individual.

Does a make-up assistant get paid?

Many make-up assisting jobs are unpaid, but the experience you gain from these is priceless. A make-up artist can learn and develop new skills and build up their speed and confidence. After assisting make-up artists for free, small paid jobs and clients are often passed onto the assistant.

How long will it take until a new make-up artist starts making money?

It is hard to say exactly as each make-up artist's career varies. It really is a mixture of luck, determination and talent. Some make-up artists may already have industry contacts, while others will have to knock on a lot of doors to be given chances, but if you are willing to do the legwork it usually pays off.

The majority of make-up artists will say it took them two to three years to start getting some better-paid make-up jobs. Remember that during this time, a new make-up artist is testing for free and spending money building up their kit, so a part-time job in the industry would be a good idea to help fund this.

How can I ensure I get work in such a competitive industry?

It is best to focus in a certain area in the industry and excel in this. As a make-up artist you will get jobs in other areas, but when you're starting out, you need to realise where your skills are best suited within the industry.

In the retail industry, your personality and ability to understand the needs of a customer who doesn't know much about make-up plays a vital role. It is important to understand that you are working with all different types of skin and ages. Product knowledge of the brand is essential and you need to know how to sell the brand by recommending the right products for your customer. You will need to have a CV and interview with the store manager and then if you are successful, you will receive formal training. There are plenty of brands to work with, so choose one that you can see yourself working with and contact the manager directly.

In TV, film and theatre, the work is regular and you do get perks such as a regular salary and benefits. These jobs are less widely available as they tend to be long-term contracts of at least six months. To get into this field, you need to send your CV to the head make-up designer and then offer to assist. In theatre, you would be expected to groom wigs and cut hair and work with the wardrobe mistress, too. By offering your services and working in other fields such as production, where you just help out and do what you can, this will help establish you as a member of the team. You may just get a lucky break, too.

The fashion and catwalk industry is renowned as being a very competitive area and how successful you are depends on your own creativity, how much exposure your profile has had and all your previous experience in working with big names.

Don't be overwhelmed. It can be frightening as your skills and portfolio are often judged before you have even had the chance met the client. The best way is to research make-up agencies and find a few artists that you aspire to be like and then offer your assistance. It really is about who you know that can get you the big jobs because they are rarely advertised. A lot of artists get their work from being recommended by a photographer or stylist or a client they have worked before. Networking at exclusive launches and parties are all vital parts of your work, as people like to see a face to a name.

Bridal make-up is done primarily for the camera and only secondly for the naked eye (the guests). The bride will continuously look back at the pictures for the rest of her life, so it is important that she looks perfect in them and, simply because on the special day, she will be the centre of attention. A traditional church wedding will require a look with soft colours, often a mix of pastel pinks and peaches, while ethnic weddings often require more vibrant colours.

It is important to have a wedding trial approximately one month before the wedding to determine what the bride wants. Work with tear sheets as the general public often do not understand make-up lingo, and these tear sheets with help the bride picture what is suitable for them.
As always, you should know what the current trends are, be able to make celebrity references, know your period make-up and understand different cultures. Keep a written and visual record of what products you have used, so that everything runs smoothly on the day.

You will either work with a hairdresser or be required to do the hair yourself, and you may also be asked to do nails. You may be requested to bring assistants with you, depending on how many people you are required to make-up, so don't forget to factor this into your fee. It is normal to expect a deposit as weddings are often booked up to a year in advance. Make sure you are paid for the wedding trial separately, in case your bride changes her mind and cancels the wedding (it does happen). Ensure you have allowed enough time for make-up application and that you have talked through your schedule with the rest of the team.

On the day, arrive early, be calm and be organised to put your bride at ease; remember this is one of the most important days of her life, so make it a special experience for her. Prepare a touch-up kit, for yourself or her to use, and be prepared for last-minute changes. You may be asked to do additional make-up on the day, or you may be required to change the make-up into an evening look for the reception.

When you are starting out, your contacts and networking are really important. Ask your friends if you can do their wedding make-up and always carry business cards. If you do a good job, you will get most of your clients through referrals. You will often get referrals from the bride or meet people at the wedding who love the make-up and are getting married themselves, or have a friend who is. Advertising in local or bridal press can help and having a website can be a real advantage. Get yourself into an environment where you can meet clients easily, a make over studio or make-up counter work can put you in direct contact with potential clients.

Afterword

"After years of writing about beauty, directing beauty and fashion shoots and working with so many talented make-up artists, I decided I wanted to put my pen down, pick up my blusher brush and get a little more hands on with make-up. This is what led me to the Academy of Freelance Make Up to train as a make-up artist.

That was a few years ago, and today I have my pen back in my hand to scribble, what I hope have been, a few helpful notes and corrections over this fabulous book and to write these final words.

Make-up artists are a thing of wonder to me. Over the years, I have watched them transform models, real women and celebrities into works of art. It always has – and always will – amaze me how beauty products can hold such power – they have the ability to instantly boost confidence, hide all manner of sins, highlight beautiful features and be the tools to create something so special that it can take your breath away.

This book shows how with creative thinking, ability and sheer determination you can become a make-up artist and when the imagination is set free, beauty can be created from beauty.

So, although I have my pen back in one hand, I will always have my blusher brush in the other."

Sarah-Jane Corfield-Smith, Lifestyle Journalist

We would like to say a special thank you to the following model agencies and PR for all their support:

Robert Hannan at Next Models. Teoh Gold at Nevs. Kai at FM Agency. Maxine Henshilwood at Oxygen. Trix Stephenson at First Model Management. Khalid El Awad and James Clark at IMG Models. Russell and Charlie at M&P Model Management models.

Aude at Christian Dior. Christina Aristodemou and Jo Scicluna at Mac Artist Relations. Lisa Nash and Helen at Shu Uemura. Jenna at Becca. Claire and Dafna at Bobbi Brown. Samantha at KMS. Caroline Young at St Tropez. Raj Kaur and the team at Lancome. Jess at purple PR. Claire at Benefit cosmetics. Alison and the marketing team at Dermalogica. Nicky at Redken. The team at Dowal Walker Pr for all their support. Jane at Illamasqua. Mary at Jessica nails. Zoe at Chanel. Candice at Balcony Jump management. The team at Blow Pr. Sophie Stanbury and the team at Swarovski. Chris Manoe and team at International Collective. Mark Whittle at No5 Cavendish for use of location and hospitality. And finally a special thanks to Jason Mallett and Ioannis Pagonis.